UNIQUE

Winning with Extraordinary Results!

Oluwasanmi Aladeyelu

KINGDOM BOOKS

Your kingdom come, your will be done

Published by Kingdom Books, an imprint of
CreativeJuicesBooks, Singapore (www.creativejuicesbooks.com)

A shorter version of this work was originally published as *An Unusual
Woman* in Nigeria in 2006 by AC&C.

All Scripture quotations, unless otherwise indicated, are taken from
the *Holy Bible: New International Version* ®. Copyright © 1973, 1978,
1984 International Bible Society. Used by permission of Zondervan
Bible Publishers. All rights reserved.

All Scripture quotations marked KJV are taken from the *Holy Bible:
King James Version.*

All emphases added to Scripture quotations are the author's.

National Library Board, Singapore Cataloguing-in-Publication Data

Aladeyelu, Oluwasanmi, author.
Unique : winning with extraordinary results! / Oluwasanmi Aladeyelu. –
Singapore : Kingdom Books, [2013]
    pages cm
    ISBN : 978-981-07-7251-2 (paperback)

1. Christianity. 2. Christian life. 3. Success – Religious aspects –
Christianity. I. Title.

BV4598.3
248.4 -- dc23   OCN857954505

SPECIAL SALES
This book is available at special quantity discounts when purchased in
bulk by corporations, organizations, and special-interest groups.
For information, please email enquiries@creativejuicesbooks.com

Contents

This book is dedicated:

To all the men and women in the world who believe that they can win in whatever they have chosen to do; that no gender or culture, created for God's own pleasure, is inferior to another, and that there are no strata among God's people, for we find His expression in us all;

To everyone: male or female, young or old, colored or non-colored, learned or unlearned, prince or pauper; everyone anointed; everyone graced;

To all my loved ones who are busy pulling down sectarian walls and turning our godly kingdom into a city of bridges and a fortress without ramparts;

And to Motun-Olu, Bezaleel and Deborah, because you are the best and you bring out the best in me.

My greatest appreciation to God:

You are the biggest stakeholder in my life. Saying "Thank You" is a deep obligation I can't do well enough, all in one bit.

This book had numerous admirers since it was first conceived, and my thanks go out to the many people who contributed in one way or another to its success. For this new edition, I am grateful to:

My wife, for being there, nurturing the most precious thing I can ever ask for: our love; and not minding the time I had to spend getting this book ready again.

All the men of God, too, who have not only encouraged me, but also supported and cared for me and my family.

All my friends who urged me on because they wanted to see this book in print again.

Reverend and Mrs Tunde Amosun, for being such an amazing bridge, helping scores of people get to where they can become the best they can be.

Ursula Lang, for the faith you have in us and all the amazing efforts you have invested in this book because you believed in it.

Thank You.

Foreword

*U*nique is definitely an exceptional book, written by an insightful author. Reading it, I am filled with great admiration for its style and rich content. It certainly affirms Elihu's statement — that friend of Job's in the Bible who said, "It is not only the old who are wise," rather, "it is the spirit in a man, the breath of the Almighty, that gives him understanding" (*Job 32: 8, 9*). Indeed, the story of Deborah Lappidoth has never been so powerfully brought out as the author has done in these pages.

In an age where people are finding it increasingly hard to see the significance of Scripture in the realities of their daily lives, this book points us back to the Bible as being important and relevant to us all. And it further asserts the truth that there is much we can still learn today about overcoming the challenges confronting us in our time, if we would only delve into the secrets of the biblical characters who triumphed over impossible odds so many centuries ago.

Read this book patiently and carefully, and great life-changing, thought-provoking and destiny-molding nuggets of truth will leap out at you from its pages. Knowing the author convinces me beyond a shadow of a doubt that what has been written here was divinely inspired.

I therefore commend this beautiful book to you. I pray that the Light will dawn in your hearts as you read, and that you will be all the better for it!

As you start working out the principles gleaned herein, you will begin to stand out. You will be lined up with the company of unique men and women whose lives stand for what is right: those who are shining examples of righteousness in the midst of perversion; unique people making all the difference in their time and, above all, accomplishing blissful ends. This indeed is your heritage in Jesus' name!

Amen.

Pastor Paul Rotua
Kingsville Church
Lagos, Nigeria

Introduction

What exactly makes you tick?
What is it that makes you stand out
in the midst of many others?

This book will inspire and teach you
the truth about being the unique person
God has intended you to be.

*E*xtraordinary results! *That's it! That's what we all want out of life.* The need to be relevant, successful and celebrated in our own time is common to all. We all want to be associated with what's best among our own people and the rest of the world.

Yes, we all yearn for goodness and great things; but, more often than not, it seems we barely get anywhere near those lofty goals. Truthfully, most people don't get to see their dreams come true in their lifetime — and that is when feelings of failure begin to creep in. It is simply unbearable to live with the reality of failed expectations!

Why? Why can't we be all we desire to be? Why don't we have all we ought to? Why aren't we reaching our goals? Why?

Perhaps it is because, in the first premise, a lot of us lack correct comprehension, an understanding of *who* we are and *what* we have been made for — those specific roles drawn up just for us, and those places God has prepared for us to fit into. Amazingly, so many folks act as if they exist just by the mere whim of fate, confined in time and space; while some others live their lives restricted by wrongly preconceived ideas of who they ought to be.

However, it is only when we begin to see with eyes of divine vision and begin to soar above the limitations our physical lives have placed on us, that we will attain our most earnest and vital desires. And that is the truth the unique person must first accept. The human life is not all contained within the obvious. Knowing the much deeper truth is what sets us free. Everyone and anyone of us who will embrace this truth will be as free as can be.

First, we need the truth!

"What is truth?" Pilate asked. With this he
went out again...

John 18:38

You may be asking yourself the same question: "What is truth?" Let me urge you to take time to read this book as you seek to find the answer.

Do not be impatient like Pilate, who refused to be enlightened even when he came face to face with the Truth, because he was too anxious about what was happening "on the outside". He cared much more about the agitation in public than what he could have learnt indoors from the Master of life Himself. Whatever is going on "*in*" you now and hereafter is always much more important than whatever is happening around you. Some things are always better than what is in vogue.

This book you are holding now is written for everyone, but especially for those who want to know the truth about themselves, God's purpose for their existence, and the secrets of pressing in where others fear to tread. With this book, we will go on a short trip together and, I promise you, you will love every bit of it.

Here, you will learn ancient but powerful truths from great men and women of old; you will also meet very interesting people and be inspired by them; and you will uncover time-tested secrets to enable you to fulfill your dreams. As we make our way through this book, you will learn to stand up to your impossibilities, understand your rightful position, and succeed in attaining it.

As you read on, my prayer is that the Holy Spirit will break through all barriers — especially those arising from the unprofitable, innate nature of the human heart — and create in you a renewed mind. I pray that God will make you one of the extraordinary people He is raising all over the world: *"a breed without greed"*; a unique person who will quit saying, "I'm underprivileged," and will start saying, "How can we improvise and adapt positively and honestly to achieve what seems impossible to us before now?"

Love!

Olu Aladeyelu

CHAPTER 1

Holding Sway against the Odds

Who are you? A Person... a Persona... a Leader?
If you are easily forgotten, it may be because
you don't maximize the contacts you make
by the impressions you leave behind.

Give them a reason to think about you
after you've said goodbye.

Beginning with Ehud, a Left-Handed Man

Once upon a time, a man called Ehud reigned in Israel. He successfully brought God's deliverance to his people. Though he was unconventional — a left-handed man — he got the people to come on the right side of living. The record states:

> While they waited, Ehud got away. He passed by the idols and escaped to Seirah. When he arrived there, he blew a trumpet in the hill country of Ephraim, and the Israelites went down with him from the hills, with him leading them.
>
> "Follow me," he ordered, "for the LORD has given Moab, your enemy, into your hands."
>
> *Judges 3: 26-28*

"While They Waited" — Putting Your Hell on Hold!

Ehud was a man who knew how to keep devils hanging while he made his way through hell in one piece. Take your cue from him: *when the path you tread in life inevitably leads you through hell, you can only press on. This entails learning how to put your immediate troubles on hold during a long run — as well as learning that, if you have to go through a nightmare to survive a night, your only option is to walk straight on, without stopping for a cup of coffee!*

The call to greatness absolutely demands that you keep moving on, despite all you may have to go through! God made Ehud a deliverer in his time, and he did his job flawlessly. That happened because, when he had to, he went through hell without wavering. This man trampled on his oppressors and left them in a pool of their own blood; he shut them in and made his way home in one piece. How could he have done all that?

Win Your Secret Struggles

The truth is that those who aspire to greatness, those who would command enduring respect and acceptance — whether from friend or foe — must first fight and win their secret battles. You must be able to triumph over yourself when none but you and God are watching. You cannot run away from this private place where you are going to have to fight and win secret victories over your covert struggles. Secret winners are the ones who eventually emerge as "enduring champions".

Champions don't arrive impromptu; they are announced on the platforms of their secret achievements when their world eventually discerns what they can offer. The world says, "Why should we waste our time on you when you've got nothing to offer yourself in the first place? You need to set some great and true standards for yourself first before we move you from where you are to where you want to be." So first let your heart embrace what you must be.

A public pedestal without a private life ends in frustration. If you give yourself breathing space in secret, you won't choke in public.

Tough It Out

> He passed by the idols and escaped to Seirah.
>
> *Judges 3:26b*

It is okay if you meet a devil on your way home or at your front door; he just got kicked out of your house on your homecoming.

After secretly doing major damage to the enemy, Ehud pressed on despite the other dangers surrounding him. He "passed by the idols". These were an assemblage of evil deities that served as the enemy's source of strength. Yeah, the enemy may be down — but what about the enemy's inspirations and legacies that linger on from one generation to the next? Ehud went through all that too, without bowing to intimidation, getting flustered, or making concessions out of fear.

Yet, afterwards, the first place he arrived at was still **Seirah!** Literally, Seirah means "a rough place". And, yes, it is not uncommon to find emerging champions going from one rough situation to another, yet not intimidated by the odds against them or the opposition they face up to. They achieve their private feats of courage, and triumph over their internal challenges as well as their external circumstances.

It is no coincidence that Seirah was located on the hills of Ephraim: a rough climb up a rough place, paving the way to a smooth victory. It seems to me that it takes the rough to make the smooth.

Proclaim Victory

> When he arrived there, he blew a trumpet ...
>
> *Judges 3:27*

Like Ehud, there will be many occasions when you will find yourself in ugly situations even though you may have gained your secret victories. These, however, are the best times to mobilize all your energies and aim for total victory:

when all the odds still seem set against you; when you find yourself in a rough place after a private victory. When this happens, remember that every night gives way to a new dawn and the *strongest* champions arise out of the most troubled times.

Now, the best time to lead by example is when life is ugly and nobody knows the proper thing to do or the right way out.

The next thing Ehud did was to sound an alarm. It is no time to get discouraged when life gets tough with you. Instead, it is time to prepare to make some noise because you are just into the last round of your bout. Amazingly, the closer you are to the end of your troubles, the tougher it gets. And, towards the end, the only tactics a failing and falling opposition has against anyone are intimidation and terrorism.

These are the idols you meet along the way, in Seirah and all the other rough places. Don't ever concede defeat to that bunch of hungry and already-mystified devils! Just sound your alarm by making some good noise! Proclaim victory by showing right examples! Scream if you want to! Sooner than ever, it will be time to exhale. Don't be intimidated or stumped by adversity when you are on the verge of victory.

Wisdom demands that you don't just sit down and watch in the face of your fast approaching victory — which often hides itself within the intimidation you are facing and those rough situations you find yourself in. This is the phase of your life when you know that you have gained victory over the enemy in a secret encounter, yet direct and external circumstances seem to give the lie to that victory. Now is the time when you have to give it your best and all you can. Now is the time to scream for life!

The time to actually proclaim victory is when you have dealt with the enemy in secret, yet on the outside the situation is still rough. This is the time to announce and decree victory. Champions like Ehud will not mind raising an army against hell, even when the going gets rough, as long as they have been able to beat down the enemy in their own home. The enemy's home is your secret life. That is where he audibly expresses himself. That is where victory or failure begins. Ehud obeyed Jesus' law, as the record states:

> "How can anyone enter a strong man's house and carry off his possessions unless he first ties up the strong man? Then he can rob his house."
>
> *Matthew 12:29*

Imagine this warfare strategy. It can only be carried out secretly. First things first: never allow your army to break in on your enemy, until you have successfully beaten him hands down in his own home — which is your secret life. Before we move into a red zone, we must be sure the enemy within is defeated, or else we might fall into his hands.

Ehud actually did more than Jesus asked. He not only tied up the strongman, he silenced him to death. Thereafter, he escaped through a dangerous route and landed in a rough place. He made a great noise afterwards; he called for the plunder of the adversary. He was indeed a great man who championed a great cause in his day. Unfortunately, after him, Israel backed out again.

Ehud was forerunner to a woman who came after him. That was because, after him, the people stopped obeying God, and another enemy came to oppress them for twenty years. At that time there lived a woman leader by the name of Deborah. She not only existed, she *reigned*. She held sway in an even more exceptional way and in circumstances tougher than Ehud's.

After Ehud died, the Israelites once again did evil in the eyes of the LORD. So the LORD sold them into the hands of Jabin, a king of Canaan, who reigned in Hazor. The commander of his army was Sisera, who lived in Harosheth Haggoyim. Because he had nine hundred iron chariots and had cruelly oppressed the Israelites for twenty years, they cried to the LORD for help. Deborah, a prophetess, the wife of Lappidoth, was leading Israel at that time.

Judges 4: 1-4

The Enemy's Advantage and Deborah

Deborah was in charge when the enemy was in better form. After Ehud died, God betrayed them to the enemy because they had sinned. When we fool around with sin and disregard God's injunctions, we are facilitating divine rejection. Every time we grieve God by doing what He says not to, we are giving the devil an advantage over our lives.

It is God's business to look after His own but He can't behold sin. The best way to become unattractive to Him is by messing around with sin. When we pick up those spiritual germs of immorality, we are turning His face away from us. And, remember, sin and wrong deeds thrive better in secret.

Nothing is as Destructive as Sin

When you successfully turn God's face from you, I can assure you that you are in for a horrible time with the devil and hell. Satan operates at his best when God turns His face away from our secret lives. God kept watching over His only begotten Son Jesus, until our Lord assumed the responsibility of bearing the sins of the world — and then, right away, God turned His face from His Son, darkness covered the earth and Jesus cried out:

About the ninth hour Jesus cried out in a loud voice, "*Eloi, Eloi, lama sabachthani?*" — which means, "My God, my God, why have you forsaken me?"

Matthew 27:46

Whatever had made Jesus cry out cannot be taken lightly. When God turns His face away from someone, it is not going to be restful for that person. We must come to understand how far from heaven sin can take us. When we go on a ride with unrighteousness, we are going as far as hell. The greatest pain of hell is not inflicted by the fire and brimstone there; it is the knowledge that God is not watching over you and is not, in the least, even thinking about you anymore. Now, that's hell indeed!

If you are wondering what sin can do to you — it will turn God's face from you. This turning begins imperceptibly, and then it will make you cry. That was why they cried in the days of Deborah. However, the emphasis here is not on the situation in Israel at the time; it is only pertinent for the purpose of pointing out the circumstances in which a unique woman was discovered.

Deborah the Righteous

She did not live among a well-behaved people who could encourage her to do what was right. She lived among an unruly lot, yet she was a woman unmatched in rectitude. *You don't have to be like everyone else.* You can choose to be different for God. Living righteously is non-negotiable.

Many people feel the best time to be in charge is when all is right and well. But that was not Deborah's case. She was in charge when the going was tough, and when the people were rebellious and did not care about what was right, as is also the case today. *Now, the beginning of exceptional difference is simply uprightness — standing your ground at a time when folks around are compromising theirs.*

> Righteousness exalts a nation, but sin is a disgrace to any people.
>
> *Proverbs 14:34*

It takes a unique person to keep hanging out with God in all sincerity, against all odds. When everyone is saying "no" to Him, a unique person will be heard screaming "yes" to God. When the whole world walks away, people who will make a difference in their time will choose to stay back on the right side. That is the Lord's side. Choosing to be on God's side gives you an identity.

Remember Jabin, the king of Canaan, and Sisera, his military commander? With their nine hundred iron chariots, they cruelly oppressed Israel for twenty long years. Those two were brutal people. They made the period in which Deborah led Israel the worst of times. But she triumphed despite the odds against her. The question is: how did she become a champion at such a horrible time? Let's unveil the secrets of her successful life by beginning with three key questions we need to ask ourselves.

Question One: Who Are You?

> As John was completing his work, he said: 'Who do you think I am? I am not that one..."
>
> *Acts 13:25*

People who create confusion in any system are the same people who lie to others or are greatly confused about who they really are. We must understand who we are and who we are not, in a world that dictates what's "in vogue" and — if we are not careful — turns us into "look-alikes". It is important that we differentiate ourselves from the hordes of men who stir up conflict, be it conflicts of interest, purpose, agenda, or the like.

Now, my friend, can you answer this question: "Who are you?" Without giving a cock-and-bull story, without telling a lie, and without any reference to your job title, position, or the role you play in any group, job or relationship?

Deborah was human, like you and me; she had her own peculiar DNA. She was an eloquent woman who ruled on the side of righteousness against the deviants who ruled on the other side. It did not matter what wrong the opposition was doing somewhere around the corner; her stand always remained "not negotiable".

Question Two: Are You True to Yourself?

All the girls may be messing around but she must keep her sanctity. Yeah, and all the other guys may be getting saggy but he remains reliable. The question therefore arises: how much strength, faith and courage do you possess to remain true and incorruptible, in the midst of a crumbling societal system? The fastest way to lose your unique identity is to lead a lifestyle of lies, deceit and compromise.

Sisera was a warlord and his stronghold was his house of iron weapons, a symbol of ruthless power. Yet, Deborah could not be subdued because she was a person with unwavering commitment to her own true identity.

> Finally they said, "Who are you? Give us an answer to take back to those who sent us. What do you say about yourself?"
> John replied... "I am the voice of one calling in the desert..."
>
> *John 1: 22-23*

Who are you? You are what your life shows to others. What are your actions saying to people around you? If you have a problem finding out who you are, the simplest way to resolve it is to find out whose voice you represent. When the world sees you in action, what do they hear: a message from God or Satan? What are you communicating through your deeds and words? You will never be able to triumph over your troubles until you can correctly define *who* you really are.

Do not look down on yourself. If you desire to be an extraordinary person, the first thing you must overcome is a false self-concept — what some call an "inferiority complex". Ooh! That has been the undoing of many. But if you are created by God, you are not supposed to be inferior — under any circumstances, by any human definition. You are just unique. Don't ever forget that!

God did not create any kind of "complex", whether inferior or superior. If you were born of a woman and not a beast, then you were made in God's image, and you are no less or more human than anyone else. No one has the right to denigrate or belittle you. Don't fall by the wayside simply because someone has ridiculed you. Just learn to live right.

You were created for great achievements — more than what you can dream of or imagine. All you need is time. When the right time comes and God shows up on your side, much more of who you truly are will be revealed. It will not only amaze the world, it will amaze you too. You are now living with a poor frame of mind because you don't even know who you are, up till today.

"Well, then, who am I?" you might be asking. Want to know the answer? Here it is: *You are God's child; His very own.* The Bible says, "The just shall live by faith" (*Hebrews 10:38, KJV*) and not by sight. It doesn't matter how you look; God is your Father. It is crucial for this truth to sink deep into your soul. This way, you will always remember it and just believe it.

> How great is the love the Father has lavished on us, that we should be called children of God! And that is what we are! The reason the world does not know us is that it did not know him.
>
> Dear friends, now we are children of God, and what we will be has not yet been made known. But we know that when he appears, we shall be like him, for we shall see him as he is.
>
> *1 John 3: 1-2*

Discovering Who You Are in a Deeper Way

Before you start talking about discovering your purpose in life, you must discover yourself because, if you do not know who you are, it will be hard to find out the proper way of going about your life. *If we don't know who we are, how can we know what to do with ourselves?* We will not understand what our responsibilities are; we will only exist as misfits in life — square pegs in round holes.

The angel who spoke to Mary about the child Jesus did not forget to duly explain who Jesus was and what His purpose in life was to be. Similarly, with every extraordinary person whose life story is recorded in the Bible, as well as all the unique people in our own time: we are the redeemed of the Lord, justified by His works and not ours. We have not been called to work for our salvation but we have been called to work it out. Our agenda is to give expression to the divine potentials already installed in us. Believe it or not, we are God's children and we represent only His interests here in this world. That's it. That's who we are. That's what you must be, in the first place... *a child and the voice of God!*

> Therefore, my dear friends, as you have always obeyed — not only in my presence, but now much more in my absence — continue to work out your salvation with fear and trembling, for it is God who works in you to will and to act according to his good purpose.
>
> *Philippians 2: 12-13*

Question Three: Who Does God Say You Are?

You must give expression to the potential God has placed in you and you must do it now. You need not be an angel or a ghost before you can say or do something tangible with your life. You don't have to be like somebody else. And, don't be "yourself" either. Be who God says you are.

Every time you look down on yourself, do you know what you are saying? You are simply saying that God, who created you, is a failure — and He definitely is not. You must be careful how you perceive and treat yourself. *You are a child of God*! Put in a better way, you are God's voice. He is the One calling out in this wilderness of life, and you are the voice He's calling through.

I heard a preacher talk on television and she said, "The reason you are unhappy with yourself is not because people don't love you; neither is it because you don't love yourself." If I may add to that, you are unhappy with yourself because you esteem yourself either too much or much less than what God says you are. You are either a greedy or an unsatisfied individual, and that is just it.

You are who God says you are and not who you think you should be. So, all you need to do is to concentrate on who you are from God's perspective. What is He willing and planning to say or do through you? Now, I believe, you need a Bible if you don't already have one. As you read your Bible, God will speak to you more about what He wants to do in and through you.

I have met people who want to be someone else. They call these other people their "role models". Most unfortunately, the people they pattern their lives after are nothing but a bunch of volatile individuals. Most are heroes in public but human cemeteries in secret. Others are nothing but wanton abusers, celebrities who leave in their wake a trail of broken relationships, sexual sagas and other acts that point in the direction of human depravity.

Why would you want to be like someone whose public reputation is all you know? Someone you only see on walkways, on television, or in the pages of those magazines you love to read? Please, be good and great. Be a child of God. Buy yourself that unique and great identity from God, and don't sell yourself short. Don't exchange the precious gem that is you for another man's fast-fading façade.

You can never be somebody else. It is a lie of the devil. Neither should you be "yourself" if, by that, you mean indulging your carnal nature; that's the worst you can be. The best you can be, however, is what God says you are. Let the world see you the way God has designed you.

*I have the privilege to inform you that the first thing you need, to be unique and uncommon in this world, is to be **you** − from God's point of view.*

If you let yourself be the unique person God has designed you to be, you have the best chance of making your mark in this world. But if you are like somebody else, the best you can be is number two. You should not be "yourself" either, for then you would be like the man who beat up his beloved wife black and blue; and, when he was queried, he said remorsefully, "That's just me and that's what I do when I'm angry." Hmm!

We permit so much dysfunctional behavior because we want to be "ourselves" and not what our Maker says we are. There is a picture God holds very dear to His heart about you and me; it looks very different from all the mess we have made out of being the non-complying and ungodly "me". We must aspire to be who God says we are. Neither what the world has to say about us nor the descriptions we make out for ourselves will do in our quest for genuine self-actualization.

Express Feelings Effectively

I have also met some sanctimonious people and all I can do is wonder: why don't they just stay over there in the opium of their "spirituality", and let those remain here who understand what it means to be real men and women filled with the Spirit of God? Unique people have feelings too, but they show them appropriately. They know when, where and how to express their emotions. Those other "super-spiritual" people, however, do not seem to have human hearts or any form of blood in their veins at all. They pretend not to have attractions, fears or other feelings common to mankind. They come across as oh-so-pious but I think they are just the opposite — hypocrites!

Usually, we respond to a situation according to the way our minds interpret it. Instead of being in control of ourselves, we are often carried away by our feelings. But there is a better way:

> So he made a whip out of cords, and drove all from the temple area, both sheep and cattle.
>
> *John 2:15*

Here, Jesus was angry with the merchants He found in the temple but He didn't just explode immediately. He took time to make a whip; He didn't get furious and start fighting everybody at once. He waited until He was fully ready to make it meaningful.

The shortest verse in Scripture reads, "Jesus wept." He wept for the death of His friend Lazarus (*John 11:35*). But He didn't just burst into tears at once; He waited till He got to Lazarus' tomb, and there His tears proved His love for His dead friend. Your actions must be tailored to achieve the right objectives. Be real and express your emotions appropriately. You cannot allow your feelings to dictate your actions all the time; yet you can't deny you are as human as anyone else.

Deborah, She Has a Name

The first thing you will observe about Deborah is her name. The Bible introduced her by mentioning her own name first, before any other reference was made. She had an identity. She was somebody before she became Mr. Lappidoth's wife. She was Deborah and she was proud of it.

What's your name? If you take some people's full names and remove from them their spouses' or parents' names, what remains becomes insignificant. Some become non-entities when they are out of an office or a position. How pathetic!

Unique people have the answers to life's riddles; therefore the world does not ignore them. They are not necessarily acting like the best around but they are full of greatness. Unique women don't throw themselves at men; they don't take solace in having a relationship with a big whip in town but, instead, men count it a privilege to be with them. They are precious jewels of inestimable value.

Now, you could be doing just fine on your own terms. That's good! But yielding to God's Spirit will always make you better. When I say, "Who are you?" I am not asking for your father's name or what you do, but *the Spirit by which you live.* I don't care what your credentials are. All I want to know is *you.* Who are you?

Listen! Only great minds avoid the status quo and improve on what is being done. They raise the bar to the next level. *Who are you?* Are you the kind of person people love to talk about after they have just met you — or are you someone who is just so quickly forgotten?

If you are easily forgotten, it may be because you don't maximize the contacts you made by the impressions you left behind. Give me a reason to remember you thereafter.

Outstanding People Bring Value to Others

> She is worth far more than rubies. Her husband has full
> confidence in her and lacks nothing of value. She brings him
> good, not harm, all the days of her life.
>
> *Proverbs 31: 10-12*

Simply because of this woman, her husband had access to
value. How do we define value? Simple! It is something that
is significant, useful and desirable to a party or person. It
could be tangible or intangible. Good health is valuable; so
are a good life, a warm relationship, a loving family, a happy
home, and meaningful work. Be a person who adds value
into the lives of others. This is what makes you significant.

> When his master saw that the LORD was with him and that the
> LORD gave him success in everything he did, Joseph found
> favor in his eyes and became his attendant... the LORD blessed
> the household of the Egyptian because of Joseph. The blessing
> of the LORD was on everything Potiphar had, both in the house
> and in the field.
>
> *Genesis 39: 3-5*

The world needs people like Joseph. He brought God's
prosperity to every place he went, be it a home, prison or
palace. The weight he carried, his significance, did not
depend on his job title, his position, the place he was in, or
his social connections. It flowed out, not through any
external glamor, but from the concealed life within him —
from an internal Grace, the Spirit of God within him.

If your concealed life meets with your public life on the
streets of London, Lagos or New York, will they recognize each
other at all? Does the value you bring flow out of an internal
Grace or is it mere bravado? Are you sure you are not just
creating empty impressions? Look at this next verse carefully.

Beloved, I wish above all things that thou mayest prosper and be in health, **even as thy soul prospereth.**

3 John 2, KJV

Friendship with God

If there is anywhere you need to add weight, let it be in your inward person. Connect yourself to God as much as possible and you will never cease to be a significant person wherever you go. Jesus wondered if He would still find faith on earth when He returned. The instability and unfaithfulness that plague human beings today was evident to God a long time ago, but you can still be unique if you would only choose to be different and to be in friendship with God. This is what you must do, to begin with, if you want to be exceptional.

You do not need to pretend you are from Jupiter or another planet different from this one. You do not need to hide your weaknesses or to deny that you have human failings too, like everyone else. You need only to yield to God's provision for your life. More importantly, *you really must be "born again"* by accepting and confessing Jesus Christ as your Lord and Savior (if you have not already done so). Any truly born-again Christian would be willing to help you with this. Please find one; if need be, you can contact me too (you will find the contact details on page 235 of this book). God loves you and it is vital that you ask Him to come into your life and be a part of it.

Finally, public shame is inevitable for people who lack a personal identity, notwithstanding their professional, political or religious credentials and affiliations. Ever heard about the lone devil who single-handedly embarrassed a seven-man deliverance team? Not a single person in that team could properly identify himself. They were seven in number, and they had a public reputation — not because of who they claimed to be, but because of who their father was.

Dr. Luke, who wrote the Book of Acts, could not identify by name even one of those boys. He knew them only as "the seven sons of Sceva, a Jewish chief priest" (*Acts 19:14*). They derived their identity only from their father's name and his position in the Jewish system. People may be held in high regard because of the group they are affiliated with or because of the things they do in that group; but in real life you speak only for yourself. You cannot function with another person's identity. Who are you... before it is too late... *one day?*

> **One day** the evil spirit answered them, "Jesus I know, and I know about Paul, **but who are you?**" Then the man who had the evil spirit jumped on them and overpowered them all. He gave them such a beating that they ran out of the house naked and bleeding.
>
> *Acts 19: 15-16*

A Persona

What is the difference between your person and your persona? Your "person" refers to "who you are", as has been defined earlier in this book. Your "persona", on the other hand, is your public identity: a combination of your character, what you do, and what is expected of you in your particular situation.

One of my friends defined character as a collection of behavioral, mental and moral qualities that go to make up a person and distinguish him or her from others. She said, "You cannot exchange character for charisma; they are two different things. Your character speaks volumes about *you*, more than all you can preach in a lifetime using all your charisma. It's like a glass; even a little crack shows all the way. Those close to you know who you really are by your character." Conversely, those who are not know you by your charisma.

In this book I have defined persona as a combination of character and charisma. As much as you need *you* — your person — you also need a good deal of character and charisma to be a part of this world and to get along in any organization. Mister or Miss Character is better understood on a private date while Charisma is the public person.

Deborah, a Prophetess

She was Deborah, a person with her own identity. But she was also a prophet of God, and that was her office. She communicated the mind of God, and that was her persona.

What do you stand for? The things you stand for, and how you stand for them, determine your persona. What are you doing with your life, and how are you doing it? Do you advance the truth or do you bring contempt to it?

If you don't stand for something, you will fall for anything. If you are not standing, you are surely falling.

Unique people do great things greatly; they do not expend their energies on gossip or tale-bearing; they live above petty hatreds and do not need to dominate over others.

Deborah was a prophet; she gave expression to what was true and divine. She was a person who felt the pulse of God's heart. You can be sure that when she spoke it was not for self-aggrandizement or public applause. She was tuned to God's frequency and spoke what she heard from Him.

Eagles don't flock together; they only cluster around in midair when the occasion presents an opportunity to lock in on their prey, or when and where there is food. When you see a gathering of great people, you know the occasion that calls for it is as important and gratifying as the guests.

Unique personas know how to stand on their own, independent of any affiliations. It is only low-flying birds that flock together, migrating aimlessly from coast to coast. We should rather be like the eagle — the great bird that soars in the air with all profundity, dignity and strength.

Don't waste your time going everywhere, when there are only a few important places you need to get to. Don't waste your time doing just anything, when there are specific tasks you must seek to accomplish. Don't waste your time babbling, when there are so many important things to say. Finding out exactly what it is you have been called to do, and doing it, will help you live a focused life — without being in competition with yourself or others.

Yes! You Can Do It!

Deborah was a prophetess — a woman prophet in a male-dominated world. But that did not stop her from accomplishing what she was called to do. You should never be intimidated by what the world considers to be "on the wrong side of the tracks" — whether you belong to the "weaker" sex, have the "wrong" skin color, or are in the "lower" strata of society. If your heart is set on something, you will do it well — even better than your so-called "betters". Unique people will have great success in whatever they choose to do; hardly will they be discomfited because of their gender, stature, race, socio-economic background, or anything else that may seem to put them at a disadvantage.

Deborah was able to reign successfully alongside two powerful opponents, Jabin and Sisera. This was not an easy feat; she had to be a strong person with a strong persona to maintain her influence over the people even when the going got rough, and her opposition was not only tough but also cruel. She was like this other woman in Proverbs 31:

> She sets about her work vigorously; her arms are strong for her tasks... She is clothed with strength and dignity; she can laugh at the days to come.
>
> *Proverbs 31: 17, 25*

She had a task to accomplish, and she was filled with strength and the unique abilities needed for the job. It is better not to do anything at all than to do it without the required will and vigor. Unique people will do what they have to do with all the required enthusiasm. You do not have to take on more than you are capable of. If you have to do something at all, then you must be enthusiastic about it, and it cannot be beyond your God-given strength.

Many people are held back by fear from achieving all that they are capable of. They need to believe that they, too, have been given "arms strong for their tasks"; that where God calls them, He also enables them. Then, they can walk tall because they know they have what it takes to make it.

A Prophetess, the Wife of Lappidoth

> Deborah, a prophetess, the **wife** of Lappidoth...
>
> *Judges 4:4*

There is yet a third attribute: Deborah was a woman, a prophetess ... *and a wife*. She was married.

One of the errors of our time is the contempt shown by many for the marriage relationship. Marriage between husband and wife is the climax to, and the most intimate of, all human relationships. But, these days, it seems to be taken much too lightly or considered overrated.

When God said it was not good for man to be alone, He definitely was not trying to be funny. If He said it was not good, He meant it was bad. Now, I am not condemning people whose marriages have broken up — no, not at all — although I won't deny the truth that such are victims of Satan's end-time scheming against humanity. Nonetheless, we can all rejoice in God's ability to work all things out — even broken marriages — for our good, for all who will keep their faith in him.

Where family relationships — especially between husband and wife — have failed or are strained, it is our responsibility to work towards reconciliations that restore wholeness to the family unit. No doubt this is a tremendous challenge today; but not to do anything would be to play willingly into the Enemy's hands.

Breaking up our homes and bruising people's hearts are the sly strategies Satan is using for a much bigger purpose: to destroy our dignity and our social framework. If the home system is destroyed, there is no future whatsoever for our society. If the home is shattered, sooner than we think, our world will become an arid place. Marriage is the right foundation of the home and we must not only respect it but also make our stand for it, in our own interests.

Your Marriage Is Important to God

> For this reason a man will leave his father and mother and be united to his wife, and they will become one flesh.
>
> *Genesis 2:24*

God went through the whole process of creating Eve for a simple reason emphasized by Genesis 2:24. He wanted to accentuate the importance of marriage.

> May your fountain be blessed, and may you rejoice in the wife of your youth. A loving doe, a graceful deer — may her breasts satisfy you always, may you ever be captivated by her love.
>
> Why be captivated, my son, by an adulteress? Why embrace the bosom of another man's wife?
>
> *Proverbs 5: 18-20*

Infidelity is in every sense a crime. Both men and women deeply detest it; we decry it publicly, yet it is being made to seem fashionable and inevitable in the world today. It is noteworthy that the man in Proverbs 5 was exhorted to remain faithful to his wife. Prayers were even offered for him so that he would gain satisfaction from his own spouse alone. Why? It is because adultery brings down God's fury on man, without Him having to lift a finger! The whole of ancient King David's family had to suffer for his infidelity. Today the world suffers unknowingly from this menace.

> Another thing you do... You weep and wail because [the LORD] no longer pays attention to your offerings or accepts them with pleasure from your hands. You ask, "Why?"
>
> It is because the LORD is acting as the witness between you and the wife of your youth, because you have broken faith with her, though she is your partner, the wife of your marriage covenant.
>
> *Malachi 2: 13-14*

Marriage is a covenant between a man and a woman. God respects that covenant and He will not condone those who ridicule it. Consider this passage from His Word:

> But since there is so much immorality, each man should have his own wife, and each woman her own husband. The husband should fulfill his marital duty to his wife, and likewise the wife to her husband.
>
> *1 Corinthians 7: 2-3*

Note, too, that the Bible forbids same-sex marriages.

> Do not lie with a man as one lies with a woman; that is detestable. Do not have sexual relations with an animal and defile yourself with it. A woman must not present herself to an animal to have sexual relations with it; that is a perversion.
>
> *Leviticus 18: 22-23*

It is only a man who should have a wife and it is only a woman who should have a husband. Anything apart from this is pure debauchery and will incur God's wrath in due time.

The Book of Genesis says that when God had finished creating everything, He declared that all He had made was good — except for one thing. He said that it was "not good" for Adam, the man he had formed, to be alone.

The Creation and Formation of Man

> So God created man in his own image, in the image of God he created him; male and female he created them.
>
> *Genesis 1:27*

> When God created man, he made him in the likeness of God. He created them male and female and blessed them. And when they were created, he called them "man."
>
> *Genesis 5:1b-2*

The "man" God was referring to in the Bible (*Genesis 1:27*) was not just the male, but the male (Adam) and female (Eve) together. It was Adam who referred to Eve as a "woman" (*Genesis 2:23*). Actually, God called her "man".

Genesis 1:27 recorded man as "him" and later as "them", meaning more than one: that is, "him" and (who we now refer to as) "her". When the Bible talks of man it is not necessarily signifying the male only; more often than not, it refers to the male and female together.

This concept will seem complex until you begin to examine Genesis Chapter 2, starting from verse 4; only then can you really understand *Genesis 1:27*. Genesis Chapter 2 sheds more light on the concept of the created man. Verse 4 begins by saying, *"This is the account of the heavens and the earth when they were created"* — and a little further along in that account it was recorded how *"the man"* was formed:

> The LORD God formed **the** man from the dust of the ground and breathed into his nostrils the breath of life, and the man became a living being.
>
> *Genesis 2:7*

The Bible referred to man using the definite article, *"the"*, not the indefinite article *"a"*. This means he was a person already mentioned or potentially existent at the time of formation: that is, the formation of his physical body.

Before that formation, man was a living spirit. After the formation, he became a living spirit as well as a human being. The man did not have a bodily form until the Lord formed him from the dust: in verse 8 it says, *"... and there (in Eden) he put the man he had formed."* Now, God is not flesh and blood but man is. However, man in addition to being flesh and blood also has a spiritual side to him. When God said, *"Let us make man in our image"* (*Genesis 1:26*), it means that the created man is not only flesh and blood but spirit too; this is so because God is Spirit.

We were created in the image of God, so we have a spiritual component. However, we were also formed of flesh and blood, and this is what makes us very unlike God. God is not flesh and blood but Spirit. There are two sides to every human: the created man and the formed man. It was the created that was later made into the formed man. The created man therefore existed before he was formed. It is the human form that returns to the dust, while the created man — the spirit — returns to God (*Ecclesiastes 12:7*), who is the Father of all spirits.

The purpose of distinguishing between the created and formed man in the foregoing paragraphs is to help you understand God's concept of man, and His views on how we should relate with the opposite sex and with people of our own sex; and, through these insights, to help you further discover your unique identity. In *Genesis 2: 7-17* we read how only the man Adam was formed, until in verse 18 God revealed a lack, a need in this man.

Why It Is Not Good for Men to Be Alone

The LORD God said, "**It is not good** for the man to be alone..."

Genesis 2:18

God Himself said it was not good for the man (him) to be alone. God made "them" male and female; and He is surely the only One who knows why He formed the male first and the female only later.

God never intended in His creation plan to make just the male. From the outset, He had already created the female version, which was also called Man. So it shouldn't come as a surprise when God said it was not good for the (male) man to be alone. He had intended all along for the man to have, as his companion, the female that He would also form. So, before the problem became obvious, God already had the solution ready.

What followed immediately after that assertion, "It is not good for the man (him) to be alone", was a pageant. God brought all the beasts He had created to the man Adam and presented them to him. He flaunted every one of them before Adam and got him to give names to all of them; but, at the end of the exercise, smart Adam did not deem it fit to call any one of them "woman". He did not say to any of the beautiful animals, "Now you are bone of my bones." But, after a long process, a conclusion was drawn with a simple statement:

But for Adam no suitable helper was found.

Genesis 2:20b

Here, you can see what the Creator was doing! It had to be *her*: **woman!** As long as *she* was not available, the man could not find his completion: a *"suitable helper"*. Whatever else we have found or will yet find is delusional. The real intention behind the pageant was to pave the way for a suitable helper to be formed for Adam — and not to be merely a naming ceremony for all wildlife.

The simple, impeccable and perpetual foundation God was laying for us here is this: of all God's creatures, however beautiful, friendly, *Your chances of losing are high when you play solo on a team that is designed as a two-man squad.* intelligent or excellent they are, none qualifies to be man's companion, not even the man himself. No substitute can take the place of a woman in the natural order of life. Not your dog, nor your cat, nor a monkey, nor any other lovable creature. This world is a man and his woman's world!

In God's eyes, another male or an animal does not qualify to be a man's "intimate" companion; and vice versa for a woman. Otherwise, He would not have seen anything wrong with Adam living all alone, having those other "guys" from the animal world as his intimate relatives. I believe God created male and female but delayed the advent of the female for a sole purpose: so that we may understand how important women are in the divine order of life.

Contrary to what is believed in some quarters, women are not necessary evils. They are necessary companions: *"helpers"*, to be more precise. A woman is the best-qualified candidate to be a helpmeet to man, to fill the role of "a part opposite; specifically a counterpart or mate" (*Strong's Hebrew Dictionary*).

Here, I am speaking to the men: *do you need divine favor?* I have an idea that can work for you, if you are in a position to marry. Go ahead and get yourself *a wife*. But, remember, she must be a wife and not a mistress or just anyone through whom you can give expression to your sexual longings and moral unruliness. Yes! She must be a woman, yet she has to be **a wife**.

> He who finds a wife finds what is good and receives favor from the LORD.
>
> *Proverbs 18:22*

What about Same-Sex Marriages?

God knew from the beginning that men would one day grow so debauched as to start flirting around with animals. He knew that the time would come when the enemy would gain evil possession of people and put jinxes on them by stirring up in them burning desires for same-sex relationships and other anomalies of like manner. He therefore left us a record of the truth in Genesis, so that we can be sure of knowing what's right from what's wrong.

What more can we expect when Satan gains possession of the human mind! If pigs went berserk when Satan took charge of their minds (*Mark 5: 11-13*), why won't men? To any man who takes another man as a "marriage" partner, or any woman who does likewise with another woman: I would only encourage you to have a deep rethink; think it through. And, for your own sake, let the truth filter into your heart because, unless the truth filters through, you will never have a change of heart — which is what your Maker really wants. You can't ever change your own mind about this in the most logical situation without the light of the truth. The whole world has gone wild today because people have rejected God's sovereignty over them. They ditched His idea. Humans have either rejected the truth outright or failed to pay attention to what was written in the Maker's user manual for the formed Man.

Let's just ask ourselves this question: would you and I exist today if marriage between two men or two women had been the norm from the start? Insisting on having it the way you like it is being self-centered. And that is what continues to destroy the essence of our mutual existence.

There is contempt for the marriage institution everywhere. Consequently, abuse abounds. Families have fallen apart; hearts are broken and lives devastated; children are fast becoming delinquents, addicts and gangsters. Rebellion has become the order of the day. Whether out of desperation or despair, some — and they can start as early as the preteen years — now go to school with guns to terrorize other children. The obvious result of all this is that it has become increasingly difficult for individuals to find and understand what exactly is the true meaning or purpose of their lives within our world's individualistic frameworks.

Marriage is a beautiful thing when we enter into it the way God intended, embracing and accepting it as truth and in truth: that it is God's plan to join a man and a woman as one in holy matrimony. Such a marriage forms the bedrock on which is built a loving family and home; and a great home is non-negotiable for the upbringing of great souls who will later mature and contribute richly in their own unique ways to the spectrums of human society. It is much easier for the home to make or mar a person's identity, purpose and destiny, than it is for any other social system.

Now, maybe you don't believe in marriage — or maybe you subscribe to the idea of homosexuality and same-sex marriages? I am afraid for you, because I am convinced you are living wrongly and are in grave danger now and in the hereafter. You are a victim of grave delusions. To me, your convictions reveal that you are suffering from a grievous psychosomatic disorder; though, for this reason, I cannot despise you. But then and worse still — you really need to know this — I believe you are part of an evil that is not new to man, of which the Apostle Paul also spoke of forthrightly:

> Do you not know that the wicked will not inherit the kingdom of God? Do not be deceived: Neither the sexually immoral nor idolaters nor adulterers nor male prostitutes nor **homosexual offenders**… will inherit the kingdom of God.
>
> *1 Corinthians 6: 9-10*

Marriage must command honor from all who are of sane mind. Homosexuality, bisexuality and bestiality are wicked acts that draw down the wrath of God. If those who engage in such deeds refuse to repent, God's judgment is inevitable: despite every legal or social claim, every political or religious affiliation, God will judge the sexually immoral in His own time. He has done it before and is able to do it again.

> Marriage should be honored by all, and the marriage bed kept pure, for God will judge the adulterer and all the sexually immoral.
>
> *Hebrews 13:4*

Now, this does not imply that if you are unmarried you are guilty of wrongdoing. It is all right to stay single as long as you do not advocate the rejection of the opposite sex or live a sexually immoral life contrary to God's idea of matrimony.

It may not be obvious whether Paul was married but, from the constant counsel he gave to wives and husbands, young women, men and widows, it is clear that he encouraged and did not deride the idea (see, for example, 1 Corinthians 7: 2-5, 9, 12-13; Ephesians 5:25-33; 1 Timothy 5:14).

If you are against the marriage institution, Satan has definitely deceived you, and you need to be set free from those lies today. Nothing in this world is qualified to be joined with a man in marriage except the one who was created alongside him and formed from him: woman. I would like to encourage all who have abandoned the family ship to go back home to their spouses (especially!) and children — today.

Let God reconcile your hearts to each other in true love and restore your marriage relationship. That way, you can help the world become a better place much more than by travelling round the globe with charitable intentions that probably won't last beyond your trip.

> So the LORD God caused the man to fall into a deep sleep; and while he was sleeping, he took one of the man's ribs and closed up the place with flesh. Then the LORD God made a woman from the rib he had taken out of the man, and he brought her to the man.
> The man said, "This is now bone of my bones and flesh of my flesh; she shall be called 'woman', for she was taken out of man."
>
> *Genesis 2: 21-23*

When Eve was presented to Adam, he gave a great shout of ecstasy: "This is it!" *This is what I've been looking for, and she is just exactly like me!* He recognized her immediately for who she was: "This is **now** bone of my bones"; implying, *No more questions, no more doubts, no more searching. This is the real thing!*

You need to be glad about that person in your life; he or she is a great blessing, if only you could perceive it clearly. Indeed, for every man that God has created, He has also created a woman just for him, intended to be his helpmate — an "angel" in human form. There are two vacuums in everyone. One is made for God and the other for your spouse. We can't survive without the former; it's hard to live without the latter. I believe in love: *the strong and tender love between a man and his wife!*

> A wife of noble character is her husband's crown, but a disgraceful wife is like decay in his bones.
>
> *Proverbs 12:4*

> He who finds a wife finds what is good and receives favor from the LORD.
>
> *Proverbs 18:22*

No wonder Adam was excited at the sight of Eve! Who would not want to find what is good? The problem is: there are women of noble character, yes; but there are also the other kinds. A lot has gone wrong from the time of creation till now. It is painful to realize that not every woman will make a good wife; and not every man will make a good husband either, these days. The whole process of finding a suitable husband or wife is a much more formidable task.

As far as God is concerned, a wife is a good thing. So too is a husband. What then is the problem? The only problem might just be with finding the right one for you.

How to Get the Best

Adam looked carefully as God paraded before him all the creatures He had made. It must have been a daunting task to name them all, one after another. What was the purpose of the whole exercise? It was to find the best companion for Adam!

But it failed to produce the desired result because "for Adam no suitable helper was found." (*Genesis 2:20b*)

Trying to find a spouse among a multitude of creatures would weary anyone out in no time. After Adam had done his best and nothing had worked, God gave him anesthesia. When God sets to work, He starts by calming man's restiveness. The best that Adam wanted came to him when he was fully relaxed, to the extent wherein God could work on him. God took a bone out of him and he couldn't even put up any form of resistance.

The best things in life are not what we can buy but the gifts God gives us. And the best gifts from God do not come when your wits are working overtime. They come when you are calm enough to allow Him His way; when you forget about all that

You will come to a dead end unless you allow God a thoroughfare in the first place.

hustling and allow God to be the Captain of your ship.

Wise men may come from the east, the west, or anywhere else; but, like the star of Bethlehem, real direction comes from God. No matter how wise they were, if they didn't follow the star, they would miss the way. In many ways, human intelligence has unfortunately become man's greatest undoing, when it is not subject to divine influence.

We tend to lose track of our true purpose when we stray out of divine direction. The little mistake the wise guys from the east made, when they consulted King Herod for direction instead of God, resulted in a situation where soldiers started killing babies. Maybe you too should stop running or jumping around! Yes! Maybe you should just relax! And let God be in charge.

Get the One God Gives

Before you start your search for a spouse, first and foremost, you must have an accurate and sufficient understanding of your inadequacies; second, you must own up to the challenges they bring; and, third, you must not be ashamed to receive help. These steps went a long way in helping Adam to handle the challenge of finding his wife.

Furthermore, don't just slip into a relationship with someone who happened to show up around the corner. You need to make sure that what you get is what God gives. Don't be so crazy for love that you jump at every offer the world throws at you. Many today still make the same mistake that Jacob did. They are so much in love with "Rachel" that they can't wait to go on a honeymoon with "Leah". Don't be like Jacob, who did not check out Laban's package for him. He just took it and went on!

Jacob was so love-crazed that he rushed into bed with the wrong woman. That still happens today. Who are you involved with? Who are you getting married to? Have you confirmed if this is what you actually bargained for? May you not discover that what you have for now labeled "love" turns out to be "folly" after the wedding night!

You can meet anybody in church or elsewhere and decide to get married; but only God can help you find the one He has for you, among all the beautiful women and eligible men out there.

Deborah, a Noble Wife

A wife of noble character who can find? She is worth far more than rubies. Her husband has full confidence in her and lacks nothing of value. She brings him good, not harm, all the days of her life.

Proverbs 31: 10-12

We cannot begin to estimate the honor Deborah brought to Mr. Lappidoth's name. She was a unique person, a prophetess *and a wife*. I am sure she did not neglect her husband or children despite her person and persona. Her husband could trust her and, as far as he was concerned, there was nothing harmful in having a woman of her caliber as his wife. She was definitely someone who made her family proud of all she was and all she did.

It is absurd how many people appear great in public... until you see how much destruction goes on in their homes. They come gorgeously dressed to church. Some reverence their pastors like God but won't even give their spouse a simple regard at home. Some sing beautifully in the choir but, when they get home, what you hear are sinister rhythms, melodies that are capable of destroying anyone who cares to listen.

A unique woman is a wife like Deborah, a wife of noble character: who brings good and not harm to her husband in private as well as in public; whose husband finds pleasure in her; and who is honored and celebrated for who she is to her family. *Do you have a family that is proud of you as a woman or man?* Consider this question well before you answer it. If your answer is "no", why is it so? Is there anything you can do on your part to make a change? Please do not hesitate to put things right today! It's so vital to you and your world.

The place of a wife, like that of a husband, is a place of duty. It was a duty assigned to the first woman and the first man, and by inheritance it is ours today. You may feel you have failed but I want you to know that past failures don't have to matter anymore. Just accept that God is not done with you yet. There is place for hope and change. A victorious person is not one who has never failed before. Successful people have their own past failures too, but they refuse to remain failures.

Tough times don't last but tough people do. Anyone who has failed in the past but refuses to remain a failure is actually unique. Mr. Lappidoth was obviously proud of Mrs. Deborah Lappidoth. Your spouse should be proud of you too. You can make discoveries that bring about breakthroughs in technology, economics or government, or in society at large. You can be a great helper, companion and partner. You can be a homemaker and bring up wonderful children. Your family should look up to you. You should not hesitate to rise up to the challenge to be unique. It's all up to you! What will you decide?

Women Who Shape Destiny

You may not be a prophetess like Deborah or a queen like Esther, but you can be the one who brings illumination to "his" mind; you can expand "his" horizon and be the queen of "his" heart. You may not be known all over the world or have your name emblazoned in newspaper headlines; but you can have a good reputation in your own home, with your name written in gold on the hearts of your own spouse and children.

You don't have to be the "celebrity" at every social event, when your home is full of love and joyful celebrations. All you need is to understand your place and duty as a spouse. Whether you are single or married, you have duties to fulfill.

The duties of a single man or woman: you are a child and servant of the living God. The duties of a wife: you are a companion and helpmate to your husband. The duties of a husband: you are a pillar of strength and a fortress for your wife. Without either of you, the job won't be well done and life would be tedious. The duties of a mother: the future is conceived in your womb and nursed with your care. The duty of a father: the future is molded in your hands. We have been given the power to determine the colors of years to come.

Perhaps you are now thinking, "But I'm not a leader like Deborah, nor as brave as her." Listen! A homemaker is a nation builder. Make your house a godly home; love and care for others. People from your home and people you have touched will go to places you have never been to, places you may never get to. When they get there, they will speak your language and impart your values to those around them. Then, you will have left an indelible mark on the sands of time, because of the impact you made in your own small world.

> Her **children arise** and **call her blessed; her husband** also, and he **praises her.**
>
> *Proverbs 31:28*

Called to Lead

> Because he [Sisera]... had cruelly oppressed the Israelites for twenty years, they cried to the LORD for help. Deborah, a prophetess, the wife of Lappidoth, was leading Israel at that time.
>
> *Judges 4: 3-4*

Furthermore, although Deborah was a wife, she was also called by God to be a leader. She was a timely leader, for she was "leading Israel *at that time*" — at that difficult time when the Israelites were oppressed and needed a strong, wise and God-led leader. She did not lead when the circumstances were easy. She led in turbulent times that would try any leader to the limit. And she came through with flying colors. With God's help, she led the Israelites to victory over their enemies.

Now, who is a leader? He or she is someone who takes charge of getting things done through the willingness of others, and for the benefit of all and sundry. A leader is a motivator of good intentions, setting the pace for others to follow; and to get people to follow, a leader has to establish credibility.

Credible leaders are those who display integrity and courage. It is integrity that inspires trust in others; wise people will not follow anyone they cannot trust. And, it is courage that inspires respect; a regiment will not follow a chief who backs out in the face of an opposition's insurrection. Cowards can't lead and, when they do, it is an entrapment for those who follow.

Leaders must be able to encourage themselves in the face of discouragement.

It is important to emphasize these three points: first, before you can lead successfully, you must have proven yourself to be trustworthy and competent; second, before anybody will follow you, you must first be a blessing to them; and, third, you must be ready to offer them something in exchange for the value they will be adding to your cause.

Deborah was a blessing to the Israelites; she was always there for them. True leadership is continuous and consistent in action. Deborah touched the day-to-day lives of her people in a positive way. She did not show up today, only to disappear tomorrow. She did not fizzle out somewhere, just to re-appear elsewhere. When the going was tough she did not run out of steam; she got tougher! She did not run to hide in an asylum when it was bedlam in her country. She was a visible and audacious woman.

There was something very different about the period of time in which Deborah led Israel. It was a time when the people had disobeyed God and were under the subjugation of an iron-fisted ruler — a tyrant! It was a time of distress and depression, but she showed up anyway and also led the way out. She stood out for her willingness to assume responsibilities that were weighty and irksome.

A unique woman indeed.

Unique men and women are those who are willing to assume leadership responsibilities wherever the need arises, whether in the most difficult circumstances or the humblest situation. Leading entails positively directing and influencing others in the right way, being answerable to them, and setting a good example. It is never an easy task.

Leading means bearing a weight; it implies living with a burden which is not even yours.

Leading Means Shouldering Responsibilities

The day when ancient Israel's leaders made a mistake and forgot to be responsible, it bred disaster.

> They set the ark of God on a new cart and brought it from the house of Abinadab…
>
> When they came to the threshing floor of Nacon, Uzzah reached out and took hold of the ark of God, because the oxen stumbled. The LORD's anger burned against Uzzah because of his irreverent act; therefore God struck him down and he died there beside the ark of God.
>
> *2 Samuel 6: 3, 6-7*

Let's get this straight: we are not called to aid or shore up a regime operating on wrong systems. We are called to take up the responsibility of leading. We are the exact system upon which the ark of God must be carried.

Uzzah's intention must have been a good one but his behavior revealed a violation of the clear instructions the Lord had given for handling the Ark. Those instructions required that the Ark be carried on the shoulders of the Levites and not in a new cart. In responding to Uzzah's action, God gave a dreadful and stunning reminder to David and the people: that those in positions of leadership must take the responsibility squarely upon their own shoulders and with the utmost reverence for God's principles. They must personally bear the burden of leading, just as Christ, the Leader of leaders, has done: "the government will be on his shoulders" (*Isaiah 9:6*).

We are the true leaders. We are not supposed to sit back; we are supposed to go all out to show the world how to do it right, because people out there truly do not know the "how to". They have not been taught, as we have, about Christ's way of leadership.

Leaders don't have light shoulders; there are always heavy burdens to bear. Deborah was leading Israel and the people came to her to settle their disputes. Her words were brave and powerful, and she commanded obedience from all. She knew the mind of God because she was a prophetess. So, her directives carried God's authority and audacity. At one point, she summoned a man into her presence and communicated God's message to him:

> She sent for Barak son of Abinoam from Kedesh in Naphtali and said to him, "The LORD, the God of Israel, commands you: 'Go, take with you ten thousand men of Naphtali and Zebulun and lead the way to Mount Tabor. I will lure Sisera, the commander of Jabin's army, with his chariots and his troops to the Kishon River and give him into your hands.'"
>
> *Judges 4: 6-7*

But Barak said to her:

> "If you go with me, I will go; but if you don't go with me, I won't go."
>
> *Judges 4:8*

And what was Deborah's reply?

> "Very well," Deborah said, "I will go with you."
>
> *Judges 4:9a*

Leadership is not about getting into a high position or achieving prominence. It is much more than getting ahead of others. Leadership means assuming responsibility for others and supporting them all the way, as much as you can, in their successes as well as failures. That was what Deborah Lappidoth symbolized. It all goes up or down with her. To be a unique person, you need to make sure the buck doesn't get past you.

Leadership Traits of Jesus

Jesus Won His Secret Battles

> Again, the devil took him to a very high mountain and showed him all the kingdoms of the world and their splendor. "All this I will give you," he said, "if you will bow down and worship me."
> Jesus said to him, "**Away from me, Satan!**"
>
> *Matthew 4: 8-10*

Like Ehud, Jesus won His secret battles. He saw vividly what the devil had to offer, and it was a great deal. But it was not enough to persuade Him to grant concessions to the enemy; he did not waver from His purpose of destroying all the works of Satan. He didn't bow to the enemy in secret.

Jesus won a secret battle against the lust of the eyes and the deceptions of glamor. It is noteworthy that any sleaze that climbs up the ladder of leadership with you will bring you down, most probably when you are at the peak. Any compromise you make in private will disgrace you in public.

A true champion is a secret winner before ever becoming a public icon. You must lead an upright life when the spectators comprise only you, the devil and God. You don't learn how to win when you are already in the public eye... you do that first, in your private life.

He Proved His Worth

> Leaving Nazareth, he went and lived in Capernaum, which was by the lake in the area of Zebulun and Naphtali — to **fulfill** [*i.e. to prove*] what was said through the prophet Isaiah... From that time on Jesus began to preach...
>
> *Matthew 4: 13-14*

Jesus did not become a champion overnight. He started from obscurity. When He began His ministry, He was alone. He did not wait for the crowds to come first; He took the initiative and started ministering to people. He proved His worth, and you need to do the same. Industrious people prosper in whatever they do, no matter how insignificant it may seem at the outset. You can start building your empire from a rat hole.

He Went for a Walk

> As Jesus was **walking** beside the Sea of Galilee, he saw two brothers, Simon called Peter and his brother Andrew.
>
> *Matthew 4:18*

Jesus took time to look around. He did not sit at home hoping for the best to come His way some day. The disciples did not come to His home; it was He who went looking for them.

Until you learn how to lay your hands on something real, you will never be ready to take charge.

God has assigned some people to you for a purpose, but they will rarely come knocking on your door. You need to get out of your shell and go look for them. You need to go on outings, attend meetings and social gatherings, and learn to relax around good and effective people. Then, take your time to observe closely. That person you need might just be around the corner. So, go out and make some good friends.

He Observed

> As Jesus was walking beside the Sea of Galilee, he **saw** two brothers, Simon called Peter and his brother Andrew...
>
> Going on from there, he **saw** two other brothers, James son of Zebedee and his brother John.
>
> *Matthew 4: 18, 21*

How well do you use your eyes? Jesus observed people before He made His move. He did not just stumble upon someone and immediately invite him or her to follow Him. Note the word "as"; it implies "in the process of". It was a deliberate process of walking, observing, and then making a decision.

Jesus did not go out walking for the fun of it. He meant business, and he went out on business purposes. Every step He took was purposeful. He enjoyed the walk but His real mission was to search for men who would later become the great Apostles of faith.

Apart from God-given revelations, you may not be able to discern a stranger's character at first sight, unless you take your time to observe him or her. Jesus took time to watch His disciples doing what they did best. His comrades were not a bunch of rascals or mere idle people. They were not gadabouts with nothing better to do than roam about town looking for new excitements. Whatever walk of life they came from, they were men to be reckoned with in their profession — be it fishing or tax collecting.

He Asked People Out

> "**Come, follow me,**" Jesus said...
>
> **Jesus called them,** and immediately they left the boat and their father and followed him.
>
> *Matthew 4: 19, 21-22*

When He called, they came. There was something about this Man that elicited obedience; something so compelling about His call that these fishermen left their boats and parents willingly and immediately. They must have been glad that the Lord had chosen them; that's why they jumped at His call as fast as they could. It was not because He had a macho personality or divine power that could draw men to Him, but because He was the quintessence of all that they desired. Jesus is someone anyone would love to meet. Are you?

Whatever you want to accomplish, start off by being a person who attracts others. You can't afford to alienate people if you hope to achieve great goals.

First, win your secret battles and become a true champion on the inside; this will attract people as they discern what you have to offer. Then walk up to the ones you have found to be eligible, and ask them out. It will be great if you can do that — but even greater when God gives them to you, and they come on board to join your team.

If you don't get down on your knees in secret to win your battles, you will always flop in public. They will shout, "Go back home!"

He Offered Something Better in Exchange

"Come, follow me," Jesus said, "and I will make you fishers of men." At once they left their nets and followed him.

Matthew 4: 19-20

They were fishermen until they met Jesus and He offered to make them something else — fishers of men. He was offering them something better in exchange for what they would have to give up, to follow Him.

Let's have a simple check here! If I decide to risk my life and all I have, to follow you today, would I be glad to have done it or would I regret it later? Do you have anything to offer that would be of interest to me? How great is your game plan? What's in it for me? What are you offering your world that we have not seen before? These men were fishermen and they knew nothing about fishing for men; but the greatest leader of all time said, "I will make you fishers of men." What excellent thing can you teach and help others do?

Here's another simple question for you. If God were to give you followers today, what would you make out of them: dwarfs or giants, slaves or freemen, scum or saints, dullards or leaders, beggars or givers, rebels or lovers, sinners or winners? How well can you manage these alternatives?

You can quickly find out the answer by the way you treat people around you. How do you treat your friends, your subordinates, even the waiter at a restaurant? If you label yourself "a giant among others" and we decide to make you the standard by which others are measured, can we be very sure that we will not be living in a continent of great dwarfs? How credible are your standards?

> Peter answered him, "We have left everything to follow you! What then will there be for us?"
> Jesus said… "Everyone who has left houses or brothers or sisters or father or mother or children or fields for my sake will receive a hundred times as much and will inherit eternal life."

Matthew 19: 27-29

Jesus offered His disciples something infinitely better than what they had to give up, to follow Him: eternal life and the treasures of heaven. Although you may not have as much to offer, you must still be willing to offer the little you do have.

You must be grateful to God for what you have and be willing to share it with and among others who don't have as much. Exceptional leaders are not stingy. Stop keeping the little you have; that is why you are not having more. Apart from eternal life, Jesus was ready to give His disciples a hundred times what they had to forego for His sake. If people are prepared to stake their lives for you, you too must stake your life for them.

Deborah was an all-time great leader too. She gave to Israel by volunteering her time and presence to help a friend win. I am referring to Barak, the man she called into her presence. She stood by him when it mattered most.

From Deborah to Barak

> She sent for Barak son of Abinoam from Kedesh in Naphtali and said to him, "The LORD, the God of Israel, commands you: 'Go, take with you ten thousand men of Naphtali and Zebulun and lead the way to mount Tabor…'"
>
> Barak said to her, "If you go with me, I will go; but if you don't go with me, I won't go."
>
> "Very well," Deborah said, "I will go with you."
>
> *Judges 4: 6, 8*

What God was commanding Barak to do was a big deal, for it required him to risk his life. But Barak did not have the nerve to question Deborah; instead he asked for her help. And Deborah agreed without hesitation. She was willing to risk *her* life with him for God and country.

Leadership is not about "lording" it over others; it is entails influencing, supporting and serving people. It is one of the qualities of a unique person. When the delegated task intimidates subordinates, a leader must be willing to help out. Asking for a leader's help will not be demeaning as long as the leader leads by example. Great leaders don't mind helping out. Do you?

Unique people don't mind giving a helping hand either. They don't hesitate when asked for help. As a leader, you not only instruct, you can be trusted to help too. You not only ask and take, you give as well.

Deborah offered Israel freedom from the iron men who had subjugated them when they disobeyed God. She offered them social justice too, as they all came to her to settle their disputes. She was a prophet of God who could tell them what they needed to know — which is different from what they felt they should know. You don't have to be surprised at how she led Israel; she was unique! Consider her words to Barak:

> "The LORD, the God of Israel, commands you: 'Go, take with you ten thousand men of Naphtali and Zebulun and lead the way to Mount Tabor. I will lure Sisera, the commander of Jabin's army, with his chariots and his troops to the Kishon River and give him into your hands.'"
>
> *Judges 4: 6-7*

To all who read this, I say to you: "You can triumph against the odds as these people did. God can lure your adversaries to their doom and give into your hands the armies of your foe." But you must satisfy four basic requirements:

1. You must be a godly person;

2. You must have a godly persona;

3. You must build good relationships (the greatest example is marriage) with people and appreciate them; and

4. You must dare to be a leader.

Great people are not born, they are made. You might now be in a situation that does not allow you to see yourself as one of them. However, nothing is an excuse for failure: neither traditions, nor society, nor upbringing, nor education (or lack of it). This is the truth: no great person has ever had a sweet drive-through road to success. If you were to ask any number of champions how they made it, the answer would be, "I came a long and tough way to get to where I am."

How far will you go in your quest for purpose? At one time or another, the leaders we see in the golden corridors of life today once believed when everyone around them doubted. The best among them took a step further to believe in God. They did not allow obstacles or limitations to keep them from pursuing their missions and goals. They looked beyond what was around them. They led by and in faith despite their fears. They dared to do what others didn't. This was what made them unique. Some were born in slums. Others grew out of ghettos. They did not allow where they were coming from to determine where they could go. They chose to stand out and walk tall against all odds. So can you. They led in their time. So can you.

We are not all coming from the same place, neither are we all going in the same direction. Where we all are now is a meeting point. Do not be carried away by any frivolous crowd that is around you today because they won't be there forever. They are all going somewhere; some up the gallery, others down into extinction. The important question to ask is: "Where am I going; and what am I willing to give to get there?" Otherwise, you might just as well be flushed down the drain of memory.

And, finally, you need a burning zeal in you because the zeal with which you go about your life underscores the importance of your future. The zeal to achieve your goals will drive you to overcome obstacles with determination. This world will not respect anyone whom it can intimidate, dominate or manipulate. We must stand up and stand out for what we believe in, and shun all human sleaze. When we stand in faith we will not fall in fear. See you at the next level.

CHAPTER 2

Bridging Two Different Worlds

An Achiever... an Intercessor... an Example...

An Achiever

She held court under the **Palm of Deborah**...

Judges 4:5

Deborah presided over a court of justice, and all Israel came to her to settle their disputes. Men and women came in droves — not to a man, but to a woman. It's quite possible to imagine the scene from a twenty-first century perspective: Deborah sitting at the Judge's bench while men and women, young and old alike, waited in line to speak and to hear from her. But not only that: whatever judgments she passed became binding.

The average person may never get to be as influential as this in a lifetime. It takes an achiever to command any kind of influence such as she possessed. Deborah was judge to a whole nation, not because she had a degree in law but because *she had influential rights. Those rights were predicated on compelling achievements.*

To begin with: observe the place where she held her court – "under the Palm of Deborah". That place was called by her name, so by every right it was hers. She owned an asset. It was not a government property, neither was it borrowed; nor was it identified as a gift from Mr. Lappidoth. In those days, the Supreme Court was held *under the Palm of Deborah.*

She did not bring the people and their troubles home to her family. She had a workplace that she went to and where, when she was done for the day, she signed out and got everyone to wait till the next day when the court reopened. And each day, when she walked in as the judge, all and sundry would stand till she took her place. Then she would call the court to order with the agenda for the day.

What kind of respect have you achieved? What type of influence do you exhibit?

Let's pay rightful attention to this: what Deborah had undertaken was more than a pet project. Her husband was not the president, neither was he named as a political figure; and, whether the palm was given to her or she acquired it herself, the truth remains that she owned something: an estate. There are diverse ways to estate acquisition. So many have acquired their properties through fraud or deceit; some by inheritance or through their political or social affiliations. But a true achiever's estate comes as a result of effort, diligence and investment.

True achievers are people who attain their goals through diligent effort. They are people whose hands are sufficient for the tasks ahead of them and whose progress is facilitated by personal diligence. The simple difference between an achiever and a defeatist is that achievers can confidently say that what they have is the blessing they received as the result of great work.

Deborah must have worked hard to grow that palm to the extent where she could derive shelter from it, for herself and others who came to her court. Either that or, if she had been given a ready-made palm, she must have taken good care of it, for it to flourish and shelter the court.

The Palm
The palm symbolizes industrial wealth. It is a source of multiple rich products from which humans derive many benefits. Using the example of Deborah's palm tree, may I ask you next: since you have been working so hard, what are those tangible things you can present as the result of your efforts? What legacies can you leave to those who will come after you? How does your balance sheet look like on both sides, when you sum up your assets and liabilities?

How many lives have you been able to impact positively, be it directly or indirectly? How many people have you effectively helped to achieve their potential? What is the value of your assets and investments? Now, I don't mean such things as ornaments, clothes, gadgets, cars or whatever else is in vogue at the moment. Those are all perishable items! They truly don't spell success. They have come to show how well they pass on with time.

Do you own something productive: value that reproduces value? If people were to come to you for adjudication, will they be sun-beaten because you cannot provide shelter for them from whatever it is that hassles them? Or will they be relaxed — knowing well that, if you can make it, they can too? Real achievers communicate to their world on the platform of their "palm trees": their inventions and the value they have built up. Do you have a platform from which you can tell your side of the story unrestrainedly?

People might not have met you before, they might not even know what you look like or the color of your skin; but they will know your product and your name if you make something happen for their good. Living a result-oriented life is what makes an achiever out of you. Unique people have inspiring stories to tell, and they speak not only from experience but also with obvious proofs of their achievements. For instance, someone wrote the book you are reading. You too should write one — or accomplish some even greater feat!

Considering the Palm Some More

The palm is a tree — one that's very important in the Middle East. Its fruit produce food for millions daily. Its sap produces wine and its seeds are made into food for camels and other animals. Fibers from the leaf stems are woven into ropes. The tall trunk is a valuable timber and the leaves are made into various articles. In Africa and Asia, the palm also produces oil, which is used to make household items like body creams and soaps. The palm is also a significant symbol in the Bible:

> After this I looked and there before me was a great multitude that no one could count, from every nation, tribe, people and language, standing before the throne and in front of the Lamb. They were wearing white robes and were holding palm branches in their hands.
>
> *Revelation 7:9*

> The next day the great crowd that had come for the Feast heard that Jesus was on his way to Jerusalem. They took palm branches and went out to meet him, shouting "Hosanna!"
>
> *John 12: 12-13*

The people who went out to meet Jesus were not holding roses in their hands but palm branches. *Hosanna* is a Hebrew word that means "save, we pray". When the multitude came out of town to pray for salvation, they held palm branches, which are used in celebration of victory. The people described in *Revelation 7:9* are the victorious in faith, and they too are holding palm branches.

Literally, Deborah operated in an atmosphere of triumph and victory as she held court under her palm tree. Similarly, you too must create an atmosphere around yourself that supports success. You are free to ask anyone who has nothing good to say to you and about you to shut up and pack up. It is your life and your choice. Your success depends on how well you allow God to determine the underlying factors. You can choose to be a winner.

> The righteous will flourish like a palm tree, they will grow like a cedar of Lebanon.
>
> *Psalm 92:12*

The palm is a tree highly regarded for its flourishing life. What more can be said about it? God says that it is an example of a flourishing life and that the righteous will share that same characteristic. To flourish means to exist in abundance. The palm is a source of livelihood. *Deborah had one.* It has great physical and spiritual meaning. Deborah is typical of the woman described in Proverbs Chapter 31. Look at what she did:

> She considers a field and buys it; out of her earnings she plants a vineyard.
>
> *Proverbs 31:16*

She did not just buy a garden but a field where she could plant vines. She did not just grow flowers, she grew useful plants. The Bible said, "She considers" whether it was valuable or not; and when she found it was worthwhile, she went ahead and did something positive about it. She was a thinker and an investor, a big buyer of value. She was the type who brought home fortune and not one who drained off the family wealth or ruined her family's reputation.

Don't waste your precious time and hard-earned income on what will not profit you in the future. Achievement by profitable investments is part of the mission statement of the unique person. Endeavor to set your life on a course that yields gains to you and your environment. What about becoming an entrepreneur? It's worth a thought!

An Intercessor

> And he saw that there was no man, and wondered that there was no intercessor: therefore his arm brought salvation unto him; and his righteousness, it sustained him.
>
> *Isaiah 59:16, KJV*

> "I looked for a man among them who would build up the wall and stand before me in the gap on behalf of the land so I would not have to destroy it, but I found none."
>
> *Ezekiel 22:30*

When there is none standing in the gap, the world lacks intercessors. True intercessors are those who have understood the importance of standing in the gap in the place of prayer, who are found faithfully praying for others. God said there was no intercessor, no one who would stand in the gap on behalf of those needing prayer. Our lack of zeal in praying for others keeps God wondering.

Today we have many people saying to us, "Please pray for me," but how often do we really pray for them? And how often do these people pray for themselves and others too?

It seems to me that nobody is interested in praying unselfish prayers anymore. Have you been praying for anyone lately?

Whatever it is, we begin to recover when we begin to pray, whether we pray for or against it.

These days, everyone wants to be prayed for; no one wants to do the praying. Today we have people who complain about their circumstances and almost everything else. We have people who know how to analyze and criticize others. They can tell what is what and why it is so. But there is no one who is actually praying.

How many times have you complained about the economy, the political system, the leaders, and other issues? How often have you lamented about your relationships, your spouse and children, and your work? And, how many times have you actually prayed? God prefers praying children to murmuring adults. Stop finding fault, start praying. Instead of gossiping around, why not try a little prayer now and then, and see the difference it can make?

Necessity, we proclaim, is the mother of invention. I dare to ask then: who is the father and who is the midwife? The father of invention is wisdom and the midwife is prayer. When wisdom comes with necessity to the place of prayer, invention is inevitable. *Prayer lovers are problem solvers.* An intercessor will birth great generations of men. If we refuse to take our place in prayer, we will no longer be relevant to God's agenda.

Who Is an Intercessor?

An intercessor is someone who prays on behalf of another person; someone who stands in the gap between the mortal ones and the Immortal One, between the guilty and their Judge, between the wounded and their Healer. What is prayed for may or may not directly or indirectly affect the intercessor, whether favorably or adversely.

> Nevertheless El'na-than and Del-a-iah and Gem-a-ri'ah had made intercession to the king...
>
> *Jeremiah 36:25, KJV*

And he who searches our hearts knows the mind of the Spirit, because the Spirit intercedes for the saints in accordance with God's will.

Romans 8:27

An intercessor is one who cries for help on behalf of people who cannot speak for themselves; one who demands justice when the wicked and strong oppress the poor and helpless; one who cries for mercy when every other voice demands vengeance.

Who is he that condemns? Christ Jesus, who died — more than that, who was raised to life — is at the right hand of God and is also interceding for us.

Romans 8:34

Even now my witness is in heaven; my advocate is on high. My intercessor is my friend as my eyes pour out tears to God; **on behalf of a man he pleads with God as a man pleads for his friend.**

Job 16: 19-21

An intercessor is someone who is willing to take up very important but delicate tasks. Just like Moses, you might be the one to bear the brunt when the stronger of the parties involved decides to strike. When the Israelites disobeyed God, He wanted to destroy all of them and raise a new nation out of Moses. But Moses said no, he would rather have God forgive His people than have himself established as a new nation in their place. (*Exodus 32: 1-14*)

As one who draws nearer to God than the rest, you will need to do as Moses did. He placed a higher priority on the people he was interceding for, over his own privileges — for an intercessor is selfless, like a true friend. The Holy Spirit and Jesus Christ also function in this office.

> Therefore I will give him a portion among the great, and he will divide the spoils with the strong, because he poured out his life unto death, and was numbered with the transgressors. For he bore the sin of many, and made intercession for the transgressors.
>
> *Isaiah 53:12*

The Bible passage above speaks of Jesus. He bore the weight of the world's sins and poured out His life unto death. Subjected to gross violation of His person, He chose to pray for the ones who were crucifying Him — while they were in the very act of doing so! He gave an excuse for the wickedness they did to Him, when He could have taken it as an occasion for their obliteration.

It cannot be emphasized enough: intercession is of such strategic importance in God's kingdom! But none of us will get down praying on behalf of another until we catch the burden and feel the passion to make a difference. There is so much going wrong everywhere, everyday; but that is not the problem. The problem is, where are those meant to bridge the gulf? Where are those who really care?

> I urge, then, first of all, that requests, prayers, intercession and thanksgiving be made for everyone.
>
> *1 Timothy 2:1*

First things first: we must request, we must pray, and we must intercede. After all is said and done, Paul encouraged Timothy to attend to some matters first, before dealing with any other business; and one of the topmost priority matters was intercession.

Deborah's Strategy: between Ramah and Bethel

Intercession involves assuming the responsibility of mediating between God and people. That was Deborah's strategy; she was an intercessor for her people.

She held court under the Palm of Deborah **between Ramah and Bethel.**

Judges 4:5

Deborah not only had investments, she had a praying altar. Her fortune, to which all of Israel subscribed, was located in the place of intercession. Ordinary people have desires — and that's all they have. It takes a unique person to desire, pray and intercede until those desires become reality. Deborah was one such person. She was a bridge builder. She created an avenue where the people could reconcile with God, the place where Immortal and mortal could be on the same page.

Our utterances won't unlock and discharge power until we begin to pray and intercede.

Real prophets never quit interceding. On many occasions, it is when you talk to God about something that He talks back to you about the same thing. Deborah operated in a dimension where Heaven and earth touched each other, a platform where men and God could come and reason together. She was consistently touching Heaven and affecting her world simultaneously — this is what it means to be "*between* Ramah and Bethel".

A Closer Look at Ramah

Scripturally, Ramah (from the Hebrew root "*rûm*", meaning "high") implies a supercilious place of imposing height — a place of *pride*, a place consciously and highly prone to thinking of itself as more superior or more dignified than others. Literally, Ramah was on an elevated site: a place where men felt on top of the world, where people looked down on others, where you didn't care what was happening downstream because you thought you were at the zenith of all there was.

Ramah is the place where you are so satisfied with yourself that when God says, "Come up hither", you begin to imagine He's idiosyncratic to command you in such manner. You believe you have it made, that you are at the highest pinnacle of life. The saying in Ramah is: "There can't be anywhere higher than here; there can't be anything much more to it all; indeed there isn't any such thing as God."

However, God — the "I AM THAT I AM" — still remains the greatest and the highest; higher than all and every "I", and all the heights of Ramah. Most unfortunately, some folks never get down to accepting this truth until they are thrown off their seemingly high and lofty perch. And, when their plunge comes, it is usually a very great fall. God is the One who sits supreme above the Heaven of heavens and above all else. All who rebel always get beaten down someday, sometime, somehow!

Ramah — Pride?

The Bible shows us the evil of raising oneself to God's height and place. The first generation that attempted this ushered in a multiplicity of languages. Remember what happened to the men who built the tower of Babel? (*Genesis 11: 1-9*) Their language became confused and their common understanding was thwarted. It was in their generation that the world began to speak different languages and became multilingual.

Pride goes before destruction, a haughty spirit before a fall.

Proverbs 16:18

The most basic form of disobedience to God is to reject the possibility of a higher sovereignty than ourselves. In so doing, we are treading the paths of pride and advancing up the slippery slopes where the proud are humiliated, as we have seen happening to famous people generation after generation.

What was it that caused Lucifer to be kicked out of Heaven? The root cause was pride, the desire to become like the Most High. He wanted to be like God but he only succeeded in becoming Satan, destined for destruction in hell.

> How you have fallen from heaven, O morning star... You said in your heart... I will ascend above the tops of the clouds; I will make myself like the Most High. But you are brought down to the grave, to the depths of the pit.
>
> *Isaiah 14: 12-15*

Now, Satan definitely understood all the implications of desiring to be like God; he knew that it would lead to a disastrous fall. His attempt to be on par with God sent him packing from Heaven. It will also send anyone out of God's presence and favor. It sent Adam and his wife out of the Garden of Eden. These days it continues to send people to early graves.

Pride is the first symptom of a falling person. God abhors it. Arousing pride in Adam and Eve was Satan's strategy to get them out of God's presence — thereby plunging all humanity into decades of satanic servitude. Pride was man's first sin, not disobedience.

> "You will not surely die," the serpent said to the woman. "For God knows that when you eat of it [the tree of the knowledge of good and evil] your eyes will be opened, **and you will be like God**, knowing good and evil."
>
> When the woman saw that the fruit of the tree was good for food and pleasing to the eye, and also desirable for gaining wisdom, she took some and ate it. She also gave some to her husband, who was with her, and he ate it.
>
> *Genesis 3: 4-6*

Obviously, this particular tree had all along been in the garden but what is amazing is that, according to Scripture,

Eve had no desire to eat the fruit until the serpent told her it would make her be like God. However, instead of becoming like God when they ate the fruit, Adam and Eve became mortals with the knowledge of good and evil but without the power to tame evil and do good. What a great tragedy!

The problem is that man wants to take the place of God. Behind every controversy between man and God is man's rebellion against God. It is man's desire not to be subject to God. And this sets God against man. Today, one of man's greatest ambitions is to prove that there is no God. Why? Because if there is no God — if God is dead — then man can do as he likes. Unfortunately, God is very much alive. Although man seeks to negate His existence, God has clearly revealed Himself to the human race. He is certainly not in hiding; in fact, He abides in the very center of our souls.

Ramah Consequences

Ramah was a name used for several places in Israel, all of them on elevated sites. One of these was *Ramah of Benjamin*; it was near Bethel and close to Deborah's home. Another location was *Ramah, also called Ramathaim*; it was the birthplace and subsequent home of the prophet Samuel. Samuel's mother Hannah was childless for many years in Ramathaim, until she went *up* to Shiloh and got desperate with God for a child. Shiloh was a place of worship.

You can't worship from a lofty height. Submission is the first requirement God looks for in anyone who comes to Him. In Ramah people live as though they are on top of the world. There, they "lord it" over others. The people there do not worship. Hannah's miracle did not come to her in Ramathaim. She got her miracle when she and her husband Elkanah *went up* to Shiloh to worship God.

> There was a certain man from Ramathaim… whose name was Elkanah… this man went up from his town to worship and sacrifice to the LORD Almighty at Shiloh.
>
> *1 Samuel 1: 1, 3*

Life may not be working out for you simply because you are full of yourself. God can do nothing for you if you decide to remain in your comfort zone, your own Ramah, where all you live for is yourself and all you depend on is your human wisdom. Perhaps you have even begun to think that you may not need God after all.

God is supreme. He is the one who directs the affairs of our lives behind the scene and, as long as we refuse to go up to Him in worship, He will not help us. He sits upon His throne in the heavens, and our precious earth is His footstool. Yet, though the whole firmament cannot contain Him, He seeks a dwelling place for Himself within every person He has made. He is in the very air we breathe, and in Him we live and have our life.

A Classic Example

Another striking story about Ramah, this time the Ramah of Benjamin, is how a Levite (a member of the clergy class) and his concubine (a woman not married to him but who cohabitates with him) planned to spend a night there but attracted trouble instead.

Just imagine the scene. This clergyman was involved in an immoral sexual relationship but felt it was okay to carry on with his dissolute behavior in Ramah! This incident was representative of the decadence prevalent in the days of the Judges in ancient Israel.

> They [Levites] must be holy to their God and must not profane the name of their God. …They must not marry women defiled by prostitution or divorced… because priests are holy to their God.
>
> *Leviticus 21: 6-7*

He [the Levite] added, "Come, let's try to reach Gibeah or Ramah and spend the night in one of those places."

Judges 19:13

What would the Levite and his concubine be doing, spending the night there together, in one of those places? This story vividly reveals ancient Israel's moral corruption at that time. Even the priests were guilty of such vice, in those days after the deaths of Joshua and the elders of his generation.

Note the words, "those places". It means Ramah and Gibeah had a lot in common, for them to be coupled together in the same breath. One thing I found out about Ramah is that it was a place where "comfort" was readily available for the compromising believer, and where some houses would not mind visits at odd hours — for a certain shady purpose.

Gibeah or Ramah: one of those places that tolerated the backslider; one of those places conducive to sin; one of those places filled with wicked men. Gibeah or Ramah — yet one of those cities God gave to Israel; but in them were people who did shameful things, who were homosexuals and men who abused another man's concubine from dusk to dawn.

In our day, we also find such wicked people among contemporary believers: examples are the sect of bishops who are currently in gay unions, and other sects of Christians who identify with the perversions of the world. They have their ancestries in Gibeah and Ramah — one of those places — and soon God will visit them again.

A Much Closer Look

When they were near Jebus and the day was almost gone, the servant said to his master, "Come, let's stop at this city of the Jebusites and spend the night."

His master replied, "No. We won't go into an alien city, whose people are not Israelites. We will go on to Gibeah."

He added, "Come, let's try to reach Gibeah or Ramah and spend the night in one of those places." So they went on, and the sun set as they neared Gibeah in Benjamin. There they stopped to spend the night...

When he looked and saw the traveler in the city square, the old man asked, "Where are you going? Where did you come from? ... Let me supply whatever you need. Only don't spend the night in the square." So he took him into his house...

While they were enjoying themselves, **some of the wicked men of the city** surrounded the house. Pounding on the door, they shouted to the old man... "Bring out the man who came to your house so we can have sex with him."

The owner of the house went outside and said to them, "No, my friends, don't be so vile. Since this man is my guest, don't do this disgraceful thing..."

But the men would not listen to him. So the man took his concubine and sent her outside to them, and they raped her and abused her throughout the night, and at dawn they let her go.

Judges 19: 11-15, 17, 20-23, 25

How pathetic. Listen and be mindful: if you are not a man's rightful companion, he *will* treat you as horribly as he likes. Or why did the Levite surrender his concubine to such abuse? Did you notice how easily he gave her up to be abused in his stead? If this had been her husband — and a righteous one — he would have said, "Take me instead, and let my wife alone." Being in a wrong relationship opens you up to abuse.

Apparently, this Levite was going to Shiloh to present a thank offering or a sin offering to the Lord. But for the sunset, they could have gone on to Ramah, Gibeah's next-door neighbor; they were located in the same region. What happened in Gibeah would also be happening in Ramah... *those places.*

Gibeah and Ramah: *those places of violence, where men took advantage of helpless visitors among them*. Let no one enter into their council. Don't join in their assembly; otherwise they will abuse you and yours. They not only asked for a gay union, they raped *a priest's concubine* from dusk till dawn. Those folks in those places — Gibeah and Ramah — are the precursors of the perverts we now find among contemporary believers.

Gibeah and Ramah — they opened up convenient avenues for those who would indulge in immoral behavior. We will only make our lives susceptible to abuse by putting up there. Apart from housing wicked men, those were places where God was not feared or worshipped. They provided an environment conducive to depravity — only to the detriment of the compromising believer. In the "Gibeahs" and "Ramahs" of our day, lives are parked at the owners' risk.

Bethel: the House of God?

> When Jacob awoke from his sleep, he thought, "Surely the LORD is in this place, and I was not aware of it... This is none other than the house of God; this is the gate of heaven..."
>
> He called that place Bethel, though the city used to be called Luz.
>
> *Genesis 28: 16-17, 19*

Now, Bethel was very different from Ramah. It was a place whose identity was changed because of what was discovered in it. Bethel used to be known as Luz, and it was a city that belonged to the Canaanites: literally, the ungodly. But what Jacob found in it was divine. Running away from his past, he decided to put up at Luz; and here, in this most unexpected place, God revealed Himself. Heaven opened and a fugitive encountered the Almighty. God intercepted a cheat who was afraid of and running from his past.

Jacob saw the activities of God between heaven and earth. He saw a spiritual bustle, the movement of angels to and from the earth at Luz (which he renamed Bethel, meaning "House of God"). It had been an ordinary place until Jacob met God there. Not surprisingly too, much of your life will seem ordinary until Heaven finds expression in it. Nothing becomes truly unique until you can see God in and through it.

Until God begins to speak through your situation, whatever you say will remain mere words devoid of power — no matter how smart or how eloquent you are. Your words will make no impact because they cannot create any meaningful difference.

Bethel Consequences

Until God shows up, everything is no more than worthless.

Jacob was a vagabond who had no idea, when he stopped to rest at Luz, about the divine encounter shortly to take place there. He held the city in no high regard; to him, it was just a casual stopover… nothing special about the place. That was before he went to sleep and saw God there. In the night, God spoke to him and when he arose in the morning he was dumbfounded. He exclaimed, *"God is here and I did not know it!"*

Everything, every place, every life will remain nothing unless God is revealed in it. People will treat everything and anything lightly; it will be abused because what is greater than man — God — has not been revealed in it. It is impossible for man to find God until God has first found man. How much of God's presence do you enjoy personally?

After his experience, Jacob concluded that Luz (which he renamed Bethel) was the house of God; but was it really? No! It was actually Jacob's entry point into the realms of the Spirit. He was afraid thereafter. Why was he afraid?

Was it because he almost lost out on this great experience? Was it because he had never encountered God before? Bethel is not the house of God but the place where God's manifest presence is revealed. Bethel is the point where mortals encounter the Immortal One, the place where the Omnipresent One becomes manifestly present. Bethel is the place where what is peculiar to eternity is demonstrated within our timeframe and, more importantly, for the purpose of bringing a man out of somnolence to a positive turning point.

How Real Are Divine Encounters?

> In the beginning was the Word, and the Word was with God, and the Word was God. He was with God in the beginning…
>
> He was in the world, and though the world was made through him, the world did not recognize him. He came to that which was his own, but his own did not receive him.
>
> *John 1:1-2, 10-11*

The Bible states plainly and remarkably that Jesus existed before His physical birth in ancient Israel more than two thousand years ago. His physical birth is recorded in the New Testament, in the Gospels of Matthew and Luke. However, the Old Testament reveals that Jesus had in fact appeared on earth on many occasions before that, each time for a specific purpose.

Theologians refer to these appearances as *Christophanies* — the pre-incarnate manifestations of the second Person of the Triune God. The Bible tells of many such appearances, in some of which He was called the Angel of the LORD.

> But thou, Bethlehem… out of thee shall he come forth unto me that is to be ruler in Israel; **whose goings forth have been from of old, from everlasting.**
>
> *Micah 5:2, KJV*

A good example of a divine encounter was when the LORD visited Abraham in the heat of the day while he was sitting at the entrance to his tent (*Genesis 18:1*). Centuries later, Moses had an encounter with God in a burning bush (*Exodus 3: 1-10*). And, again, when Shadrach, Meshach and Abednego were thrown into the furnace by the Babylonian king, the LORD joined them in the fire too (*Daniel 3:25*).

When you come to your Bethel, the place of your divine encounter, you will begin to pursue a course different from the life you led before. Every one of you who comes to your Bethel will have your orientation corrected and your actions re-designated from mortal to divine purposes.

Now, Bethel (the physical place) is not the house of God because God is Omnipresent; He is everywhere and He is not restricted to any specific location or time. But your Bethel is the spiritual place where you are privileged to come into God's presence; where you meet with God one-on-one on earth. It could be by your bedside, in your car or in a desert.

I know someone who met Jesus in her room in Mecca when she was there on a religious pilgrimage; and, because of this encounter with Him, she preaches for Him today. She found her Bethel in a fundamentally Islamic nation. God is all around you, wherever you may be — even as you are reading this book. But you may never know it until He reveals Himself to you.

Religious Extremes

Jesus took Peter, James and John with him and led them up a high mountain, where they were all alone. There he was transfigured before them. His clothes became dazzling white, whiter than anyone in the world could bleach them. And there appeared before them Elijah and Moses, who were talking with Jesus.

Mark 9: 2-4

Until this incident when Jesus was transfigured, it was an acceptable practice to build a tabernacle or shelter at the site of a divine encounter. People did it, probably out of fear of not having such a great experience again or because they wanted to show the world they had this special visitation.

However, every Spirit-filled child of God — especially one who lives daily in His presence — will agree with me today that if we were to build a monument like Jacob's after every Bethel experience, we would only be stuck with our building projects and wouldn't be advancing in purpose at all. All we would have succeeded in doing would be to tie ourselves down for all time to the Bethels in our lives.

The kingdom of God is continuously on the move today. We don't have to set up a worship center and monuments in every place where we had a divine encounter; otherwise, we would have a whole lot of edifices to put up. This is because the Spirit of God is resident on earth at this present time. Hear the request of Peter and consider Jesus' reaction to it:

> Peter said to Jesus, "Rabbi, it is good for us to be here. Let us put up three shelters — one for you, one for Moses and one for Elijah." (He did not know what to say, they were so frightened.)
>
> *Mark 9: 5-6*

> But Jesus came and touched them. "Get up," he said. "Don't be afraid." When they looked up, they saw no one except Jesus.
> As they were coming down the mountain, Jesus instructed them, "Don't tell anyone what you have seen, until the Son of Man has been raised from the dead."
>
> *Matthew 17: 7-9*

Amazingly, although Peter did not know what to say, he still had to say something — anything. Some folks will never stop being a nuisance and hindrance to God's purposes that way.

The plain truth is that, where and when purpose is not yet known, all we need to do is to stay calm until we come to due understanding. If you don't keep your cool, you may miss something important because restlessness only compels abuse of purpose.

Peter must have felt, "Jesus, you see, this place is so great and just right for us. So, let's just piously stay here. Let's put up some edifices and invite the rest of the world to come around for religious tourism." He must have felt, "Let's publish what we have seen and minister to the world from here."

He must have thought of getting some workers to join him in building a castle on that spot. So, instead of moving from city to city and roaming from town to town, it would be so good to just stay there and make it a comfortable place for the Son of Man to lay His head. That way, he would have succeeded in making Jesus and that very place a sightseer's attraction for the whole world!

However, Jesus' response was quite different. He told His disciples to "get up", and they went on to attend to other pressing issues down the mountain. Here's a truth our Lord demonstrated: God gives us divine experiences, not for us to show off, but because we need to become transformed people, helping those downstream.

God reveals Himself to us primarily because He wants us to know Him better. He wants us to have a closer personal relationship with Him. Then we can live this life as God's emissaries, with the power to displace devils to the glory of His name. If we choose to stay back on our mountains of transfiguration, we will only succeed in making beautiful legends out of experiences that are supposed to reinforce our confidence in God and empower our actions among men.

Now, Deborah, an Intercessor between Ramah and Bethel: the Crucial Bridge

Now, Deborah did not live in either Bethel or Ramah. She was *between Bethel and Ramah*. She lived a life of consistently touching Heaven and affecting the world positively. She did not build an edifice, as Jacob did or as Peter suggested. She was a prophetess and, after meeting in prayer with God, she came down to be a blessing to people who would not climb the mountain of Bethel like she did.

Prayer is the middle ground. Deborah was an intercessor; she was on the middle ground between Ramah and Bethel. She bridged two different worlds: the world of Ramah, where people lived wicked lives and did not worship or fear God; and the world of Bethel, where God and man met, and where Jacob entered into the realms of Heaven.

Deborah stood between a failing and compromising world and the place of the manifest presence of God. She was a mediator by virtue of her location and positioning. The place where she held her proceedings created for her an opportunity to intercede. She was a virtuous woman and, apart from being a prophet, she was a leader — leading and judging an unruly people, and mediating between them and God. She was the crucial bridge between man and God.

The Verdict

The unique person connects others to God by praying for them. They are greatly needed to intercede on behalf of others. The distance between God and man can only be bridged by people who know how to intervene in the place of prayer. These are people who won't look down on sinners and who won't blend in with them either. They are people who will not live alone in a private heaven on earth or on a "God Reserved Area". While they have fellowship with God, they are not afraid to reach out to a dying world. Deborah was a bridge builder. She kept in touch with both God and people.

> As for me, far be it from me that I should sin against the LORD by failing to pray for you. And I will teach you the way that is good and right.
>
> *1 Samuel 12:23*

We should never get too busy to pray for our friends, our children, our other loved ones, our homes, and anything else that affects our life directly or indirectly. We should pray for our country and countrymen. Jesus even advocated prayer for our adversaries. Look in the Bible; check biographies of great men and women of God. You will find that all of God's faithful servants knew how to put their knees down before Him in prayer.

Name anyone you know: is it Daniel, Moses, Elijah, Esther or Christ Himself? They all prayed. Jesus groaned greatly in prayer, His sweat becoming as blood, all because of His endeavor to save humanity by His death on the cross. Prayer is a crucial way for us to take our stand in the spirit between God's incorruptible kingdom and a decaying society. Some of the greatest businesses that Deborah undertook included praying, interceding and mediating between God and men.

> She sees that her trading is profitable, and her lamp does not go out at night.
>
> *Proverbs 31:18*

Deborah was an investor in profitable businesses; yet she invested in prayer too. Her lamp did not go out at night. Your daytime success is dependent on your midnight diligence. We can't be idle; we must watch over our affairs very well. We must be diligent in prayer so that we can prevail over darkness even in the nighttime. So, let's pray!

And an Example...

An Example of Fortitude

> Joseph named his firstborn Manasseh and said, "It is because *God has made me forget all my trouble and all my father's household*." The second son he named Ephraim and said, "It is because *God has made me fruitful in the land of my suffering*."
>
> *Genesis 41: 51-52*

"Manasseh" sounds like the Hebrew word for "forget". The blessing of Manasseh made Joseph forget where he came from; and the man who forgets where God picked him up may also not care to be grateful for where God has placed him. He may cease to be a worshipper.

The name Ephraim, on the other hand, literally means "fruitfulness in the land of suffering". Ephraim signifies a man's ability to make meaning out of life against the odds and despite the pain suffered.

The name Manasseh signaled Joseph's intention to forget his painful past. He wanted to forget, not only his brothers who had sold him off, but also Jacob his father. Now, Jacob was the third-generation custodian of the Abrahamic covenant and blessings, for God had made a covenant with Abraham and his descendants:

> God said to him, "As for me, this is my covenant with you: you will be the father of many nations... I will establish my covenant as an everlasting covenant between me and you and your descendants after you for the generations to come, to be your God and the God of your descendants after you."
>
> *Genesis 17: 3, 7*

However, as long as there was Manasseh — a broken bond between Jacob and Joseph — what God had covenanted with Abraham could not be fulfilled. That was why, when Jacob and Joseph were later reunited, Jacob considered Ephraim to be greater than Manasseh, though Manasseh was the elder of Joseph's sons.

> Israel [Jacob] reached out his right hand and put it on Ephraim's head, though he was the younger, and crossing his arms, he put his left hand on Manasseh's head, even though Manasseh was the firstborn... [He] said, "... his younger brother will be greater than he, and his descendants will become a group of nations."
>
> *Genesis 48: 14, 19*

Jacob put his right hand on Ephraim, Joseph's younger son, because he was meant to be greater than his elder brother, Manasseh. Why? Manasseh was a great miracle but Ephraim, though younger, was greater. This is so because, rather than obliterating the past, Ephraim brought it to mind; the name implies the ability to be successful with God's help, where on your own you would have failed.

In naming his firstborn Manasseh, Joseph signaled his refusal to acknowledge the tribulations he suffered in times past — although it is normal to want to quickly get over an ugly past. But, by naming his second son Ephraim, he became an example of a man who acknowledged God's ability to give him victory despite the odds. And it is upon such platforms as Ephraim represents — fortitude in the face of suffering and setbacks — that you will find unique people. They serve as good role models to all they meet.

Inspiring by Example

Deborah was an inspiration to the young. The simple message that always got across to people who met her was: "If Deborah made it, so can I." Her successes and experiences were not shrouded in secrecy. On the other hand, something about her life always brought hope to the hopeless and light to those in darkness. That was the example she set.

She held court… **in the hill country of Ephraim**.

Judges 4:5

She did not reside on a mountain of transfiguration, secluded from the world and forgetting how far she had come to get to where she was. She held court in the hill country of Ephraim, the place of victory in the midst of contentious lawsuits. She remembered from whence she came, and thanked God for where He had brought her.

Everywhere Deborah went, people loved to hear her story. She was the quintessence of hope and faith; she had the guts to build wealth out of rubble. She was a great example to her world.

Leading by Example

"You are the light of the world. A city on a hill cannot be hidden. Neither do people light a lamp and put it under a bowl. Instead they put it on its stand, and it gives light to everyone in the house. In the same way, let your light shine before men, that they may see your good deeds and praise your Father in heaven."

Matthew 5: 14-16

Deborah, a prophetess… was leading Israel at that time.

Judges 4:4

Deborah did not hide herself away; hers was a very visible and strong presence. She held court in Ephraim; she was the judge and leader of a nation. The world could see and hear her as she passed her judgments on diverse matters and made major state decisions. She was a light shining in the darkness of her world.

The best form of leadership is by example. It would be foolish of me to follow you on a route you yourself have never taken, in spite of any promise you make that it will lead me where I want to go. This is because you are not God. He is the only one familiar with all the routes of life. He is the only one who knows every detail about every road because He made them all. He knows what is best for you and me. And, because He is faithful and all-powerful, He is the only One whom we can always trust to do what He says He will do for us.

The only grounds for my attempting to trust you are based on the examples you show me. The best we can do is to take the road first before we lead others down it. Let us set a good example, at the very least! Then we have something to offer to those who follow.

What kind of examples do you proffer to your world? What does your trademark look like? What difference does it make? This is what really determines the kind of person you are, whether you are unique or ordinary. No unique person ever led but by example.

Notwithstanding how well you can talk people into doing something, they will always want to see how good you are at it yourself. Are you sure what you have is worth sharing? Are you sure you are teaching the world what is right, whether through the books you write, the music or movies you make, or the television programs you host? Consider it; is all you have to offer not mere trash? I would suggest that you start today to create good products and services that build people up. Products and services sell with little advertisement when they are useful and offer good value. How reputable are your claims and what difference do you make to your world?

CHAPTER 3

Praiseful and Peaceful

A Peacemaker... a Prophet... a Comrade

Deborah Lappidoth Was a Peacemaker

She held court under the Palm of Deborah between Ramah and Bethel in the hill country of Ephraim, **and the Israelites came to her to have their disputes decided.**

Judges 4:5

Deborah was by nature a peacemaker. And that was why people were fascinated by her. When we envisage it exactly the way the Bible puts it, we find a whole nation — all of Israel, both the folks residing in their home country and the ones in the Diaspora — coming to this woman.

"And the Israelites came to her": the word "And" here is implicative. It suggests that a prior event led to a later one. It implies that people *came for a reason; one I have earlier mentioned.*

If you take a closer look at *Judges 4:5* again, you will discover this very important sequence: the crowd did not come just for a puppet show; neither did they come to a cinema. Rather, they came after a woman who was rightly located in a district between Ramah and Bethel, a place that gave her the privilege of being an important link between two different worlds: a place in the hill country of Ephraim, where she had built her ministry on a credible testimony.

She had the reputation of a person who had survived against the odds. Remember, Ephraim means: *"It is because God has made me fruitful in the land of my suffering."* She resided where you would find the resilient; among folks with great survival stories. She did not live among a band of rebels or with folks who got ousted easily and quickly.

All of Israel did not come to Deborah just for the fun of it. They came to calm their nerves. Indeed, it is quite incredible to have a whole nation seeking audience with just this one woman; but, if this were not so, Scripture would not have stated it so explicitly. God wanted us to see something exceptional here, and He ensured the proper keeping of those records. It was a deliberate action taken by the nation of Israel: "*and they came*". They were not compelled.

Deborah did not go canvassing for business or appointments. No one — neither she herself nor anyone else — painted her face on billboards to display all over her country. Yet people came looking for her. Let us pause to ponder on ourselves here, as we consider how attractive her life was. Is there something about you that commands an audience's attention? Or are you the repulsive individual everyone wants to keep at arm's length? There was something about this unique woman — people sought her out just as surely as butterflies seek out a flower's nectar.

What was the secret of her fascination? To put it as simply as possible, she was a peacemaker. She didn't fuel contentions or encourage rivalry. No party ever succeeded in getting her on their side of a dispute. Her judgments were never biased but objective, never partisan but always just.

When there is contention everywhere, all the unique person wants to do is make peace. That was why they all came — men and women, young and old. A whole nation was at her beck and call because they knew that, when they got to Deborah's court, they would be halfway towards reconciling with one another; by the time they left her presence, enemies would have turned into friends. That was the effect she had on them.

Leading a quarrelsome lifestyle only makes you repugnant. It is high time you started making peace with and for your world. If you are the type who loves a fight, you definitely will have to live with the dearth that comes with its frights. You cannot go on stirring up a row every now and then, and expect to be celebrated by people; the best that life can offer you will be desolation. On the other hand, if you can help nip conflicts in the bud, you will be a pleasant song on the lips of many, and you will always be welcomed.

Any enemy of peace is also an enemy of life. If you are able to stamp out strife and conflict, if you are able to reconcile people who are at loggerheads, I can assure you that the world will register its presence at your doorstep. Amongst all, you are going to be unique. Strife is the generic culture of the world. In a world of conflict you need, as a first rule, to "vote for peace as much as you can so that even if you inevitably go to war, you would be vindicated." The Bible exhorts us to pursue and promote peace:

Turn from evil and do good; seek peace and pursue it.

Psalm 34:14

There is a future for the man of peace.

Psalms 37:37

There is deceit in the hearts of those who plot evil, but joy for those who promote peace.

Proverbs 12:20

If it is possible, as far as it depends on you, live at peace with everyone. Do not take revenge, my friends…

Romans 12: 18-19

Blessed are the peacemakers, for they will be called sons of God.

Matthew 5:9

It is a great privilege to belong to God, to be called His own; and the criterion for this is to be peacemakers. Warfare is never a better option; it is always a disastrous resolution that creates more trouble than it ever hopes to solve. Let God fight the battle, if there must be one. What man has achieved so far with war is a waste of precious human lives, especially those of innocent children and helpless women — all in an effort to impose one's will on others.

Every warmonger, notwithstanding his or her credentials, status or position, belongs to the devil. Listen! Deborah did not go around making problems for and with other people; she only resolved the ones they made for themselves and others. You have a choice whether to make war or peace; and, furthermore, the extent to which peace is allowed to reign depends so much on you and your fortitude to withstand and not give in to provocation.

A Prophet: the Prophetic Grace

> Deborah, a prophetess... sent for Barak... and said to him, "The LORD, the God of Israel, commands you: 'Go... I will lure Sisera, the commander of Jabin's army, with his chariots and his troops to the Kishon River and give him into your hands.' "
>
> *Judges 4: 4, 6-7*

Now, it is not a hard thing to exist in terrible times, if you have a superior understanding of those times. Deborah reigned against the odds in her time, against the provocative "iron man" Jabin and his annoying as well as ruthless General Sisera — because she knew what God was up to. She knew God's intention was to lure the enemy to the frontline, where Sisera's weapons of war would fail against ancient Israel. That frontline was the Kishon River.

In those days, the Kishon River flowed through the northern part of the ancient Samarian hills, cascading through a plain called Esdraelon before entering the Mediterranean Sea through the Bay of Acre (known now as the modern Nahrel-muqatta). This place, to which God was luring Sisera and his chariots and troops, used to be water-logged. Most times it was swampy and marshy. Getting the enemy mired in the bog was the strategy God employed to bring deliverance to His people. It takes God to think of such a "ridiculous" (but brilliant!) idea in a military campaign.

The world is looking for answers to solve complicated life problems and break the stranglehold of wicked tyrannies. These answers can never be found in the archives of human intelligence, political strategies or military might. Wise men may come from the east, the west, or anywhere else; but true direction comes from God's Spirit alone. You may want to confirm this by exploring the secret persuasions of the men and women who have truly affected the world for good.

God is the Father of our Lord Jesus Christ; and Jesus is the ultimate Strategy by which salvation was brought to all of humanity. It was an idea that confounded the Sanhedrin, the high priest, the elites, and the rest of the Jews in Jesus' day. It confounded the whole of hell too. Some people still consider it a ridiculous strategy today. But "the foolishness of God is wiser than man's wisdom, and the weakness of God is stronger than man's strength." (1 Corinthians 1:25)

Christ was a man of peace. He has "become for us wisdom from God" (1 Corinthians 1:30) and has called us to be His peacemakers in a contentious world. The followers of Christ are the salt in this fast-rotting world; and the frontlines of their battleground are built on His peace. His peace: a boggy platform for the belligerent and those who profit from strife. His peace: an illogical strategy totally unacceptable to the unbeliever.

Power to Understand the Times and the Seasons

Victory did not come because Barak had a formidable military force or because he had better weapons of war. Victory came because there was a prophetess who taught them a superior strategy she had learnt from God.

> And of the children of Is'sa-char, which were men that had understanding of the times, to know what Israel ought to do; the heads of them were two hundred; and all their brethren were at their commandment.
>
> *1 Chronicles 12:32, KJV*

> The princes of Issachar were with Deborah; yes, Issachar was with Barak, rushing after him into the valley.
>
> *Judges 5:15*

These men of *Issachar* had and were acclaimed for superior knowledge. They knew what ought to be done. They joined Deborah and Barak in their quest for a country of free men. Now a lack of Prophetic Grace is one of the worst evils that can ever befall any man in leadership. Governments and politicians of today's world make wrong and costly decisions because they will not heed the true prophets of God or the insights that are truly inspired by God's Word. The best of ideas proffered by their advisers are but those common among the best of men — because these advisers do not operate from the divine frequency. However exciting these ideas are, they soon reveal their inherent flaws; they are unable to produce the exceptional results needed to break the vicious cycles in which the world is caught today.

God has already set the agenda for the future of the world and for everyone; what is left is for us to align ourselves with Him. Take it or leave it — either way — we and all that we are, all that we do and will continue to do, are simply the tiny dots that combine to form God's big picture.

Whatever you choose, He already has the canvas ready-made.

The qualities that really set the unique person apart from others are the exceptional information and rare insights he or she possesses and uses. Among the squad that went to war against the iron man, Jabin, were the men from Issachar. This group of men had a reputation for wisdom, and for possessing timely and relevant knowledge. Many years later, another generation of men from Issachar would also be counted among those who stood with David when Saul hunted for his life — for they too possessed wisdom and insight that told them David would one day become king over Israel.

Men of Issachar are people with divine understanding. They have unusual knowledge and are able to accurately determine outcomes — not by merely following the sequence of events in society but because they dance to divine rhythms. Their inclinations are different from those espoused by the rest of the world, especially on occasions when human intelligence is celebrated among men more than divine wisdom.

However, these men always come out as champions because they deal in and respond to the mind of God; to the prophetic. They always do the right thing at the right time and in the right company — however ridiculous it might have seemed at the onset.

A Rugged Grace... as against Sorcery

Issachar is a rawboned donkey lying down between two saddlebags. When he sees how good is his resting place and how pleasant is his land, he will bend his shoulder to the burden and submit to forced labor.

Genesis 49: 14-15

Men of Issachar will not act until they can see the future or the end of a matter from God's point of view. They are *rawboned;* characterized by rugged strength. Most times they appear to be self-effacing but they are actually one of the most potent forces on the face of this earth.

There is another spirit, however: that which fortune-tellers and the likes of them claim to be able to predict the future. This is very different from the Spirit of God. It is not the prophetic grace of God, although it entails "divination". The best that such fortune-tellers can do is to "guess" the future. God's prophets, however, don't guess; they reveal what is to come.

There is a lot of difference between guessing and revealing the future, although words such as *foretelling, predicting* and even *prophesying* have been employed when referring to both. Only God has the power to make totally accurate declarations about the future — and that is the mark of true prophecy. So, not every spirit is from God: for example, it was an evil spirit of divination that resided in the slave girl during Paul's visit to Philippi (*Acts 16: 16-18*).

Such abilities of divination have also been found in many others such as Nostradamus, "the man who saw tomorrow", as he was popularly called. This man had much to say about a world that would come many years after him. Some of his predictions appeared to have come close to the truth but they were never exact on anything. Guessing based on some facts can never be good enough grounds to build a body of truth!

Two very important characteristics of divine insight are its ability to be specific in its revelations and exact in its outcomes. This is the very nature of the prophecies recorded in the Bible: as distinct from the predictions given by the surreal and cheap spirits of divination, which are also found among fortune-tellers and mystics today. These other foretellers of the future may be smart but they are never exact or fundamentally scriptural. Their predictions are very different in nature from Bible prophecies, which are always specific and exact, and in accordance with God's Word. Examples are the revelations by various prophets in the Bible regarding the nature of Jesus' conception and his birthplace.

The Prophets Revealed

Therefore the Lord himself will give you a sign: The virgin will be with child and will give birth to a son, and will call him Immanuel.

Isaiah 7:14

But thou, Bethlehem Ephratah, though thou be little among the thousands of Judah, yet out of thee shall he come forth unto me that is to be ruler in Israel; whose goings forth have been from of old, from everlasting.

Micah 5:2, KJV

And it was verified...

All this took place to fulfill what the LORD had said through the prophet: "The virgin will be with child and give birth to a son, and they will call him Immanuel..."

Matthew 1: 22-23

When he had called together all the people's chief priests and teachers of the law, he asked them where the Christ was to be born. "In Bethlehem in Judea," they replied, "for this is what the prophet has written..."

Matthew 2: 4-5

And so, it came to pass...

In the sixth month, God sent the angel Gabriel to Nazareth, a town in Galilee, to a virgin... The virgin's name was Mary.

The angel went to her and said... "Mary, you have found favor with God. You will be with child and give birth to a son..."

"How will this be," Mary asked the angel, "since I am a virgin?"

Luke 1: 26-28, 30-31, 34

So Joseph also went up from the town of Nazareth in Galilee to Judea, to Bethlehem the town of David, because he belonged to the house and line of David. He went there to register with Mary, who was pledged to be married to him and was expecting a child. While they were there, the time came for the baby to be born, and she gave birth to her firstborn, a son.

Luke 2: 4-7

Other examples are the prophecies Jesus gave about the destruction of the temple in Jerusalem and the "abomination that causes desolation".

As he was leaving the temple, one of his disciples said to him, 'Look, Teacher! What massive stones! What magnificent buildings!"

"Do you see all these great buildings?" replied Jesus. "Not one stone here will be left on another; every one will be thrown down."

Mark 13: 1-2

The massive stones the disciple was referring to were white, and some of them were as huge as thirty-seven feet long, twelve feet high and eighteen feet wide. Jesus' prophecy was fulfilled literally in AD 70, when Titus completely destroyed Jerusalem together with its temple buildings. Those huge stones were even wrecked to collect the golden sheets that melted from the roof when the temple was set on fire. Excavations in 1968 have uncovered large numbers of these stones, thrown down from the walls by invaders.

"When you see 'the abomination that causes desolation' standing where it does not belong — let the reader understand — then let those who are in Judea flee to the mountains."

Mark 13:14

Here, Jesus was echoing a sure word of prophecy given by the prophet Daniel. (See *Daniel 9: 25-27* and *11:31.*) This explains what happened when Antiochus Epiphanies erected a pagan image to Zeus on the sacred altar of the temple in Jerusalem. Some bible scholars also believe that there are still more stages to come in the full fulfillment of this prophecy. This is possible because the prophecy is not time specific. It says *"When you see,"* and this could be anytime ... *when!*

There were also prophets among Christ's apostles and disciples in the early church. Peter, for example, knew that Ananias and Sapphira had lied about the price at which they sold their estate *(Acts 5: 1-10).* Agabus predicted the famine that would occur in the reign of Claudius. He also revealed that Paul would suffer in Jerusalem and later be handed over to the Gentiles *(Acts 21: 10-11).* That last prophecy was fulfilled soon afterwards. (See *Acts 21:27* onwards, all the way to the last chapter of the Acts of the Apostles.)

The Old Testament also records many examples of the "specific and exact" nature of divine prophecy. One such incident took place during the time of the prophet Elisha. In those days, the king of Aram was at war with Israel; but every one of his schemes was foiled because, each time, Elisha gave the king of Israel specific and exact information about the Arameans' military strategies.

> Time and again Elisha warned the king, so that he was on his guard in such places. This enraged the king of Aram. He summoned his officers and demanded of them, "Will you not tell me which of us is on the side of the king of Israel?"
>
> "None of us, my lord the king," said one of his officers, "but Elisha, the prophet who is in Israel, tells the king of Israel the very words you speak in your bedroom."
>
> *2 Kings 6: 10-12*

Elisha gave the Israelite king exact information about what was going on in another man's house, in another country. This cannot be guesswork. Neither is it scientific deduction nor a logical inference.

Foresight and Attitudes

Men of Issachar are acclaimed as rugged. They are men whose keen foresight determines their attitudes. They are not afraid to do unusual things to attain their destiny or to align themselves with God's purposes and His appointments. As a result, they can face the future boldly and take on their worst adversaries by the crosshairs. Think of it. How well will you face tomorrow, if you lack confidence about what it brings? How well can you hold on, if you lack foresight and don't even know what God has planned or promised?

A new season was coming and the tables would shortly be turned on Israel's enemies. In the past, the nation had traded sovereignty for servitude because of her rebellion against the Almighty. God would not hold on to a man who keeps fighting to break off from Him. So He allowed Israel to taste the bitter fruit of her rebellion: subservience to her enemies. But Deborah in the midst of it all knew that, in due time, power would soon change hands again. How did she know? Because she was a prophetess given to prayer; in the intimate place of meditation and mediation on behalf of her people, she had acquired spiritual understanding of her times and seasons.

While waiting on God, unique people will catch insights into God's mind that the rest of the world can never know. When the going gets tough, we get going. Not because we are really tougher but because of what we know! Oh yes! Because of what we know! We know something! And it is what we know that makes us tough in a wrecked and dangerous world.

Deborah knew the mind of God and was not afraid to speak it to the face of hell. All others might bend their backs in shame and desperation but she would always stand tall even in the hardest of times, because of what had been revealed to her by her God. Sometimes, like her, we could become bruised and broken; other times we might be bowed down on the outside but, also like Deborah, the spirit within us can never be beaten down by any disaster whatsoever. Within, she always stood tall and looked ahead. She was a prophetess. She knew the known as well as the unknown, and that kept her head up and kept her resilient.

Now, you say you have a question for me? And it is, "Is it still possible to hear God in these days and in this age?" Then my answer to you is *"Yes, my friend!" The truth is that the world can never become too noisy that it overwhelms God's voice.* If you will just calm down and keep on listening, you will hear Him. You may hear Him calling you or you may hear Him talking to you. Sometimes He will tell you to go somewhere and see someone. Most times He will ask you to read a portion of your Bible. This is not mere hallucination. You will know it is real when He shows up. And what you hear will be confirmed by the Bible.

Despite the hullabaloo the world generates, God's voice can never be drowned out; no, not by any human ruckus. When He speaks, He does not need any sound-enhancing system to make Himself heard. He speaks on a private frequency, while allowing the world to continue making its own noise. Anyone who cares to tune in to God's frequency will always hear Him loud and clear.

Folks still hear God today when He speaks. Contrary to what many believe, you do not have to be "super-spiritual" for God to speak to you. He speaks to ordinary people like you and me. The only question is: will we take the time to search out His frequency — and when we have found it, to stick to it? We can choose to listen to Him or to ignore Him. *What will your choice be?*

God is and has always been available all along. You are the one at large. Here is a sure strategy you can employ, if you desire to tune in to His frequency: go on and be committed to Him in true devotion, prayer, worship and service, and in the study of His Word. Examine the Scriptures diligently. Pray from your heart in faith and believe God is not far from you. Most sincerely I say to you, He is actually very near — nearer than you can ever imagine.

It is the devil who wants you to believe God is far away, outside your local sphere. No! In fact He is so very close by! This is a truth without any trick to it. Faith is not fiction. Spiritual truths are not vague speculations. God's Word points the true way to Life and is not an opiate for the fickle-minded. We have not been called to live an absurd ideology. What you must believe is the truth that **you can know Him if only you will choose to**.

Find a place free from distractions. Ask God to speak to you and I assure you He will. The longest distance between you and God is not even that of the nearest church to you. It is the distance that exists between your knee and the ground, the distance between your heart and His Word.

Deborah was a unique person. She was a prophetess because she knew the mind of God, and not because she wore a priestly robe; not because of any religious attire or because she held any venerable position. Forget about the façade; she could instruct her world, not because she held a political office, but because she had God's power in her, for she was in touch with the Holy Spirit. You too can be a unique person who knows the mind of God and hears directly from Him. Triumphing against the devil's lies, **you too can be a prophet**!

A Comrade

A friend loves at all times, and a brother is born for adversity.

Proverbs 17:17

A comrade is a loyal or trusted companion, a friend who is like a brother. Comrades-in-arms describe fellow soldiers who are united in executing a war against a common enemy. A comrade-in-faith is that man or woman who will not mind going the extra mile with you to ensure that you win and that you accomplish what God has designed you to achieve.

The world needs people who are willing to come alongside others as comrades. To have one and be one makes for exceptional living. Be a good friend and don't drive people away from you. A comrade is a friend who is ready to *You can always go the extra mile when the road is not a dead end.* be held responsible to a great extent for the life of another — like a comrade-in-arms when soldiers are at war. Jonathan was an example of such a comrade. At the expense of his own life, he was there for his friend David. God used him to preserve David's life. He fought for and protected his friend even though David's survival meant that he himself would be deprived of succession to the throne of Israel. (That was supposed to be his birthright, by the way.)

Comrades are more than just colleagues, roommates or partners. The ties that bind them are much stronger; it is a covenant relationship. You cannot afford to let your partners down or leave them alone when they are down. You are someone who has come to realize the truth that, if we live only for ourselves, we will also die alone by ourselves. Living well demands that we reach out to others and make a credible impact. Deborah was a friend in and to Israel.

A comrade provides strength for the weary

While David was at Horesh in the Desert of Ziph, he learned that Saul had come out to take his life. And Saul's son Jonathan went to David at Horesh and helped him find strength in God. "Don't be afraid," he said… "You will be king over Israel…" The two of them made a covenant before the LORD.

1 Samuel 23: 15-18

A comrade provides refuge for a friend in distress

"But if my father is inclined to harm you, may the LORD deal with me, be it ever so severely, if I do not let you know and send you away safely. May the LORD be with you…"

1 Samuel 20:13

A comrade provides true, but not sensual, love and affection

"I grieve for you, Jonathan **my brother**; you were very dear to me. Your love for me was wonderful, more wonderful than that of women."

2 Samuel 1:26

A comrade provides unselfish and sacrificial devotion

Saul's anger flared up at Jonathan and he said to him…"Don't I know that you have sided with the son of Jesse…? As long as the son of Jesse lives on this earth, neither you nor your kingdom will be established. Now send and bring him to me, for he must die!"

"Why should he be put to death? What has he done?" Jonathan asked his father.

1 Samuel 20: 30-32

A comrade secures and wins benefits for his friends and his friend's family

David asked, "Is there anyone still left of the house of Saul to whom I can show kindness for Jonathan's sake?"

2 Samuel 9:1

There are many buddies but few comrades, many acquaintances but few brothers, many admirers but few lovers. Satan has turned this world into a selfish and hostile place. Almost everybody is self-seeking. Where do you stand?

Apart from being great lovers, couples with successful marriages are first and foremost comrades. It is imperative that they share a common faith and do not pursue their own selfish or conflicting agenda. Close friends can share such a relationship too. Friendships that have stood the test of time are those that are unselfish and formed in a spirit of comradeship and mutual respect, aiming more for what one can give rather than what one can take!

"I Will Go with You"

> Do two walk together unless they have agreed to do so?
>
> *Amos 3:3*

> Barak said to her, "If you go with me, I will go; but if you don't go with me, I won't go."
> "Very well," Deborah said, "I will go with you..."
>
> *Judges 4: 8-9*

What powerful words! **"I will go with you!"** She did not order people around as though they were her zombies; she lent a helping hand in implementing her instructions. She was a leader who could be counted on to help; men were not afraid to ask for her help in matters of life and death. Here, a man refused to go on a mission that affected his country's destiny until he had a woman's consent to go along with him.

Deborah was a supportive friend. Women are usually expected to stand down and seek protection when it comes to warfare but, here, a man is refusing to go to war without a woman's support. Definitely this woman must be unique.

You would expect Barak to be the one all-eager for battle, and Deborah to play a stereotypical woman's role: go weak at the knees at the very mention of war. But the roles are reversed here. He said, "I can't make it without you." *She replied, "I will go with you," and that settled it!* Going the extra mile to help a friend achieve success was not too much for her to do. What she meant was: "If all you need to succeed is my presence, then you can count on it. I don't mind coming with you too, just to make sure you become a champion."

Jesus' Instructions

"If someone forces you to go one mile, go with him two miles. Give to the one who asks you, and do not turn away from the one who wants to borrow from you."

Matthew 5: 41-42

These days, no one wants to hang around nascent potentials. Everybody wants to stay on the bandwagon but that is not the real champions' route. Real winners know what it entails to prevail, to obtain, and to invest so as to acquire. Deborah and Barak won the war and returned home in exultation.

A unique person rose to the challenge and did not mind working with another who wanted to be a champion. I don't mind walking with you too, if it will bring out the champion in you. Committed friendship is a challenge we must all rise to. True friends are very rare. If what you want is a true friend, you must be one yourself: be a comrade-in-faith, willing to go the extra mile to help others become the champions in life that God has designed each of us to be...

Everything you have in life is on loan to you. You will be made to pay back only what you don't invest.

A Peacemaker

She brings him good, not harm ...

Proverbs 31:12

A Prophet

She speaks with wisdom, and faithful
instruction is on her tongue.

Proverbs 31:26

A Comrade

She opens her arms to the poor and extends her
hands to the needy.

Proverbs 31:20

Today and tomorrow, let us give to the poor and
extend love to someone who is in need —
and God will bless us real good.

We need to do this, knowing at the back of our
minds that all we have is from God; and it is a
privilege to do all we can for Him by serving
others. For every bit of our capacity is a loan from
God. *"Alas! For it was borrowed..."*

CHAPTER 4

What's Unique?

*The reason we do not command due respect
from others is that we have not been making
profound statements with our lives.*

*Live your life every day as if you are
saying something important.*

What's Unique?

Anything unique is usually held in high esteem. Common articles, on the other hand, are often accorded little respect. Such is the case with people too. There is something about everyone that others are familiar with; and this familiarity often breeds contempt. However, there is also a part of every individual that is unique: a part known only to the Creator and sometimes to the individuals themselves, and to a few perceptive people who are sensitive to the individuality in others. This is the part that makes all the difference.

What is unique may not always be new but it will definitely be different. A unique man or woman will be distinctly different from the average person; and, when you are unique, you can expect people to take notice of you wherever you go — even though they may not know exactly who you are. The moment you appear, people will immediately give you their full attention. Because of the remarkable example you set, they will get talking. More often than not, they may not even need to ask any questions about you, as all they need to know would already have been bruited about town — and my advice is simply to let them say whatever they will.

The vast majority may not subscribe to your ideals; you may not be everyone's friend; folks may not be given any assurance about your next move or agenda. Nonetheless, your uniqueness cannot be ignored. You may not be singing all the time to the popular tune of the moment; you may in fact be marching to the beat of a different drummer. But the tempo you keep will always draw keen interest and attention from people around you.

When Jesus came, Israel was thunderstruck at His teachings, His way of life and the authority He exercised. The kind and good-hearted gave glory to God and exclaimed, "We have not seen it in this fashion before." However, the heinous ill-treated Him, aiming for the furtherance of their own selfish agenda — one that was no longer in line with God's purposes. They wanted to protect their traditional reputation as Israel's spiritual leaders. To that end, they facilitated Jesus' crucifixion — but the fact remained that, in so doing, they were unknowingly furthering God's original plan. And this just about sums up the blueprint God has mapped for the unique person's life:

Sometimes what you have to go through could be a means of bringing you to where you have to get to. Those mockers around you might just be a way of letting you know you're different — and their wicked actions are fitting exactly into God's plan for you!

When something is said to be unique, it simply means it is uncommon, unheard-of in the mainstream, and much still — rare! Certainly, there are gems, but there are also *rare* gems. The rare and unique do not share equal attributes with the rest of the throng. They could appear simple but they can never be presented in the light of business-as-usual. They break conventions and boundaries, and defy the imagination of everyday folks.

When the unique emerges, it may sometimes create grave controversies and, at other times, interesting conflicts. Nevertheless, one thing pertinent about its nature is that it cannot but elicit great astonishment. Anything unique is apt to induce discussions that demand keen attention.

The Common Mind

This is the typical human mind. It is characterized by fear and indolence, and makes an enemy out of whatever it cannot subdue or grasp. It detests and challenges every mystery it cannot unravel. Sometimes, it may cynically classify a new friend as an enemy. One major reason people live redundant and unprogressive lives is that they are too quick to dismiss anything different as being an enemy.

The common mind is not dynamic or flexible; it is awfully rigid. In contrast, the unique mind opens and closes at the right times and seasons. Closed minds settle down in the house of contempt; they are always finding fault with what appears different. They prefer routine and are apprehensive of the extraordinary.

The dynamic mind, in contrast, goes in search of the unique, while the unprogressive are busy building thick and tall walls around their small, vain world. The former believes in breaking new grounds through adventure; the latter only get to hear of what is being done.

The Unique Mind

The unique mind is a powerhouse of creativity and invention. The powers that rule the ages have always been found among "unconventional" men and women. This is a paradox the most intelligent have failed to unravel. Hitherto, world changers and champions have never been the products of institutions where the common mind predominates — for example, the halls of academia. Ironically, the bulk of folks in classrooms are protégées. What they enjoy is the benefit of being taught the findings of erudite people who probably existed in an earlier time, people who were products of real life circumstances.

There is always an identity crisis in the world of common minds. They all have complacency as one attribute in common: this tendency to just sit or hang around mediocrity, in the absence of creative thinking and purposeful living. They are mostly takers and rarely givers, mostly talkers and rarely listeners, mostly onlookers and rarely doers. They would rather choose to keep on propagating archaic practices all their lives instead of daring to invent something new and different. In a world of infinite potential, they are advocates of the "final world philosophy" — *If all you are doing is what everybody wants to do, I doubt if you are living a purposeful life.* the belief that the best that can ever be has been, and there is never a need for a change in the status-quo.

Unique people, however, have discovered who they really are — their true, one-of-a-kind identity — in a world of look-alikes. They have found their distinct purpose in life, and are charting their course in a world of generalized agenda and conflicting interests. If I may ask, who are you and what is your business around here? What are you doing that makes a positive and exciting difference in the world or in the lives of people around you?

If you can tell me something about yourself that I can be passionate about, I would have met a man or a woman with the power to rule the future from the present: a world changer and a living champion. I would have met a highly unique person.

Profiles of Some Unique People

Let us now take a look at the profiles of some people who lived differently from others of their day…

Deborah lived in the days when human societal systems did not place much value on women and children, but only on able-bodied men. Yet she made such an impact on her world, so much so that generations after her continued to subscribe to her ideals. She left her mark on a world where men were used to lording it over their womenfolk. She was Mr. Lappidoth's wife — and she was one unique lady. But for this woman, her husband's name would have gone down unnoticed in history. It is amazing how great an impact such a woman can make in the world of men.

Perhaps one of the most important questions every would-be wife should ask herself is, "What can I or what am I going to make out of my man?" and not "What can my man offer me or make out of me?"

The reason why all hell is breaking loose and Satan is launching an all-out violent attack against women is now clear. If we care to read between the lines, it is now evident why these forces of hell continue to work so hard to promote, through modern media, an extremely false image of the ideal woman — one based mainly on western idiosyncrasies fixated on outward appearance and style, rather than on God's standards of inner beauty and character. It is because, in many parts of the world today, God wants to raise unique women who will bring down wickedness in high places — women like Queen Esther in the days of ancient Persia and Media.

Women can do this world a whole lot of good, much more than we yet know. Thus the need for hell to bring upon them unimaginable savagery aimed at shutting them in —

and shutting them up. But I am glad at the prospect of every woman who will learn to spread her wings and fly, just by reading this; and if you are one such woman, be encouraged to know that God is with you, and He will enable you to rise above all your obstacles.

Queen Esther was a lady who saved her countrymen from the evil schemes of the rich, influential and proud Haman. This man represents those who are in rebellion against God and who seek the extinction of other people for their own self-advancement — until they are brought to their downfall by godly women who maximize their potentials of beauty, humility, purity, prayer and fasting as Esther did. Women like Esther are the key players who function as catalysts for the advancement of God's glorious kingdom on earth.

Now, are you a woman? Would you believe it, if I told you that women are already winning out there? These are the days when you too can be a winner, if you dare to take your chances. And, are you a man? Would you accept it too, if I assured you that the triumph and ascendancy of the women in your world is not a slap on your masculinity? There are women around you who are still good, godly and faithful. Not all are "Jezebels," and not all deserve to be slighted. Though you may live in Babylon, there are yet some daughters of Zion around, and it is a shame to feel insecure because there are capable women around. It is a sign of weakness to think that shutting them up, or in, is what makes you man enough.

Mary Magdalene was another unique lady. She was the first to proclaim the resurrection of the Christ. She was a woman with a shameful background until she met Jesus. She had seven devils in her until Jesus freed her from them all;

thereafter, this woman could not tame her love for her Lord when He was all she had. She heard Him say He would die and rise again on the third day.

She saw Jesus die; yet she saw Him come to life again, as He had promised. That was because she chose to do the unusual. While others were mourning their Lord's death, drenching their pillows with the sad tears of a lost love, she walked through a dark night into a bright and beautiful morning — and into the waiting arms of her risen Lord.

She must have stayed awake all night to welcome the Savior at the breaking of that dawn. Before it was morning on the third day, she did the unusual and broke into the reality of a unique revelation.

The Mystery of the Third Day

> At that time some Pharisees came to Jesus and said to him, "Leave this place and go somewhere else. Herod wants to kill you."
>
> He replied, "Go tell that fox, 'I will drive out demons and heal people today and tomorrow, **and on the third day** I will reach my goal.'"
>
> *Luke 13: 31-32*

If we were to single out the people who worked the hardest to care for Jesus, I am sure His mother would be foremost among them. Thereafter would be His disciples. Then, the sick that He healed, the hungry that He fed, the oppressed whom He delivered, and the poor He had preached the good news to.

So when did the Pharisees begin to love Jesus? What price their profession of "love", that they would give Him security briefs concerning His life and ministry? It was definitely a ploy on their part; they were the very same people who handed Him over to Pilate.

The truth is, when you are on course to fulfill your destiny, when you are in line with God's purposes, intimidation is inevitable. The "Pharisees" around you will be envious of your prospects, especially if your purpose is unique, divine and exceptional, and if it challenges the authority of men who propagate ungodly traditions. So watch it! Sycophants do come around disguised as your friends; but in reality they are your enemies, secretly trying to destroy you. Some "loves" are nothing more than ploys to bring you down.

You need to know where your adversaries are coming from; their "good" advice is not really in your best interests but rather to serve their own selfish ends. Advice can come from anywhere and from

Purpose is what you must do with your life that is different from what everybody else is doing. It's your area of specialization!

anybody, but we must be careful from whom we receive counsel and how we react to advice given by various people.

There are times when people will claim to care for you, not because they really love you, but because God is doing something in and with your life that intimidates them or threatens their status or standing in society. You may need to take steps to shield yourself from such wicked counselors, whether they appear friendly or not. Their purpose is to tear you down, not to build you up.

Like Jesus, you too must guard against being a victim of the *"old prophet-young prophet"* syndrome. The young prophet in 1 Kings Chapter 13 had done excellently and was onto the last phase of his mission when a *"big brother"* came along and lured him into disobeying God with the simple statement, *"I too am a prophet as you are."* He believed the old prophet, went against God's counsel, and paid for his disobedience with his life.

You need to remember that Satan, too, can preach and prophesy just as well if not better than any prophet. Truly, he is the most deceptive "old prophet" of all time. And the Pharisees in the days of Jesus were a typical example of what the old prophet represented. It does not matter what anyone claims to be; do not let anything or anybody mess around with what God has set in your heart as His instructions to you.

In *1 Kings 13:24*, the lion refused to tear the donkey apart, but waited beside the young man's body. It is amazing how an animal could teach a prophet of God obedience: its application and implications. The same man who deceived the young man announced his doom. He said:

> "You have defied the word of the LORD and have not kept the command the LORD your God gave you. You came back and ate bread and drank water in the place where he told you not to eat or drink. Therefore your body will not be buried in the tomb of your fathers."
>
> *1 Kings 13: 21-22*

The lion that met this young prophet on his way home was not on a hunting exercise. It was on a mission from God and, unlike the prophet, it followed His instructions down to the smallest detail. It attacked only the man, as directed by God, and not his donkey. When the job was done, it was not afraid or ashamed to stand by it (that is, the young prophet's demise). It would not run or walk away despite the damage it had done. That was an object lesson for whoever cared to learn; it taught that when God set a man on a course, He also wanted him to stand by it.

Don't allow yourself to be browbeaten by human opinions or schemes. It takes a lion-hearted man to obey God and stand by His divine business. No matter what others may think or scheme against you, you must never allow them to distract you from your business; otherwise they will also be the ones to judge, mourn and lay you to rest when you end up losing your divine placement.

The old prophet at the sight of the young prophet's demise exclaimed, *"Oh, my brother!"* Did he forget he was his brother when he deceived him — and only remembered when he took his corpse home for burial? Don't become an enemy's brother after death and don't be buried by a stranger in an alien land because of disobedience. Don't fall because you had more reverence for human opinions than for God's injunctions.

The Pharisees' report about Herod was intended to throw Jesus off course from His timing and purpose. As far as Jesus was concerned, Herod was no better than a scheming fox. Anyone who threatens your life or your divine purpose is no better than a wild dog from God's point of view.

In times past in Europe, foxes were kept for hunting. The animal was proverbial for its cunning. There are some human foxes too. These are the people who hunt others down and scheme against them. They will use all sorts of hoaxes and manipulations to try to distract you from pursuing God's purposes for your life. If Satan tried to hunt Jesus down, no one among us will be exempted.

If God has set you on His course, I encourage you not to be afraid of what man can do to you. You cannot be taken out until you have fulfilled your purpose. Everyone who understands the power of God in divine placements knows that human threats are paper lions that don't bite us out of our divine destiny. Every time you are threatened, look the devil in the eye and scream, "You can't get to me as long as I am connected to God's purpose! Until, like Jesus, I have come into my third day; when I can say, like Paul, that death in Jerusalem is not a failure!" Feel free to let Satan know that he can't intimidate you because God is on your side. Paul didn't only get to Jerusalem; he also went on to preach in Rome after his arrest in Jerusalem.

On a Divine Assignment

There is nothing like being on a divine assignment, living your life to the full for God. That is when you will not be afraid to go out, when the ovation is at its loudest. The prophet Agabus came to Paul, tied his hands and feet with the latter's belt, and said, *"Whoever owns this belt will be thus bound in Jerusalem."* Paul's reply was like, "That is not a bad thing, you know; it is okay to die for Jesus after living this much for Him." (*Acts 21: 10-15*)

You see, it's so amusing that Satan does not have the power to take any of us out until God is ready to take us in. So, what's your fear all about? You can make a big fool out of the fallen angel if you know what you are doing and your place in God. Yes, the devil is full of tricks; but he is predestined to be a failure.

The third day is the season of triumph for us. We are not going anywhere until we are done with our goal, until our dreams are all fulfilled. If the enemy couldn't scare the Lord out of town until He was done, he shouldn't be able to scare us out either. We must keep on. You may be threatened, mocked, harassed or abused. You may be ridiculed but you must keep to your purpose and not quit until you have gotten to where you were made for. Don't burn out too soon!

The world may not accommodate you, and you may have to sleep outside all night long; yet you must not give up until you have closed in on your victory. The whole of hell may go on rampage around you, but you must ensure that you do what each day demands of you. Although you may not yet be there, you are on the verge of reaching your goal. You must keep moving even if all you can do is drag yourself to the finishing line. The issues of the first day and the successes of the second day are nothing compared to the glories of the third day. Just go on, and on, and on!

If you believe that by the power of God you can achieve your dreams, you must receive this truth. The enemy may threaten you now but you must not be afraid of paper lions. It may look like your life is at risk but the truth is your life is on the rise, climbing ever upwards.

You must keep doing something tangible today and tomorrow and, on the third day, you will shine like a star in the sky. You must keep contributing the little you can now, because you are going somewhere. You are not just hanging out. You are not a scoundrel. You are pioneering greatness.

Be bold and walk tall. Inform as many as possible about your emerging victory. Don't be afraid to say, "Wait for me, I am coming out gloriously on the third day"; and even if they won't wait, you will be proven right on your third day if you keep pressing on.

Friends may desert you as Jesus' disciples did: Peter decided to go fishing and James and John followed suit. But it didn't matter. Jesus still rose from the dead on the third day. You too will have your day of victory anytime soon! If you will persevere and not back out because of the threats from within and without, if you will not give up because your friends stopped believing in you, you will soon showcase the glory of God in your life. You will honor Him who has the power to bring your dreams to life — on your third day, when your time for celebration comes.

At the dawning of your third day, you will bring the right answers to the night's struggles. Jesus provided the same fish His disciples struggled to catch all night long, but couldn't. Read the following Bible verse to yourself again and again, and get convinced you are safe and will be coming out a winner despite all odds:

> "In any case, I must keep going today and tomorrow and the next day — for surely no prophet can die outside Jerusalem!"

Luke 13:33

Jerusalem is the king's city: the home of champions, the palace where true princes dwell. It is the command center where crowns are received and thrones established. Every great person must report there in due season. They come around on their third days for great celebrations. God is never done with anyone; no, not until they have found their place in Jerusalem, the metropolis of champions — until your life calls for a celebration.

On the third day after Jesus' death, **Mary Magdalene** went to say "Good Morning" to an apparently dead man in a crypt — a man who had in fact already risen from the dead — and the rest is a story we all know. Until we decide to do the unthinkable, that which everyone else scoffs at, we may never break into the unimaginable that will amaze the world. When we come into an alliance with Heaven — that is the day we are ready to rise above every human imagination. Sincerely, I say to you, it is only in the realms beyond human imagination that you will find the emancipation of unique people.

Everyone wants the job done but no one wants to knuckle down to the task. And, so, we may never see any progress until a unique person comes along — that is, the one who will get going at once and do what needs to be done; the one who will wait only upon God and not for someone else to come along to do the job.

The Syrophoenician woman is another unique person who got her miracle against all odds. She didn't mind being insulted; she was called a dog but she said, "It's okay! *Just get the devil out of my daughter!*" She successfully put up an argument that Christ admired and endorsed, when He hurled Satan out of her child. Are you also tenacious enough to fight and win your case against anything or anyone who threatens your precious ones? You bet *I* am!

Her thrust was this simple: "It is not only the children who know how to eat bread; even the dogs can eat bread well enough. And sometimes a dog can be smarter than children. If the children don't take care and won't come to the table fast enough, before the show is over, the dogs may have disappeared with the food that the children refused to eat at the right time."

Jesus acknowledged that this woman's faith and her arguments were unique. So she got the bread. Her daughter was freed! She won!

It is high time we woke up and kicked complacency in the face. Heaven is waiting. God is actually in search of His people, to make available to them their rights in Him — but the question is how long will He keep looking? I hope you will not be out of town when God calls at your house.

You don't want to give dogs any occasion for taking your place in God's plan, do you? Why should you be here on earth as God's child and He have to take an alternative route, like going through the unbelieving, to achieve His goals? We can't allow rocks to take our place when we have the honor of living for Him. God will always accomplish His purposes, whether He is allowed to use us or others. He has made us His preferred route but we have a choice whether to grant Him thoroughfare or not.

The woman with the issue of blood is yet another with unique faith. She successfully interrupted Jesus' schedule. She took up His time, delayed His trip, and got His healing power flowing into her body. In spite of her fears and amidst the common throng casually touching our Lord, she reached out with a unique, purposeful touch of faith (*Mark 5: 25-34*).

Hers was no casual encounter; she meant business with God. She had to fight her fears: she was considered unclean by her culture because of her ailment; and it was unacceptable for her, a woman and an unclean one at that, to touch a man, and a holy man at that. This notwithstanding, she mustered her faith and overcame the enemies of doubt and fear within, so she could overcome the enemies without.

She must have rehearsed her lines well before she stepped up to her Lord. She was a woman with a bloody issue; but her resolute mind and her one touch of faith resolved the issue for her. *Her mind was resolute before she came on the scene.*

She said to herself, "If I only touch his cloak, I will be healed."

Matthew 9:21

Champions must first speak into themselves before they can start speaking to and with others. You need to continue to speak words of faith to yourself until they become your powerful resolutions, lodged deep within you. What you profess should not be mere words but beliefs that spring forth from the depths of your heart. You must first convince yourself before you try to sway others. It is only then that you can go ahead and start proclaiming those great truths that spring from your own convictions. That's how it works!

The way we go about our lives must send a strong message to the world. The Bible says, "As soon as they hear me, they obey me." (*Psalm 18:44*) The reason we do not command due respect from others is that we have not been making profound statements with our lives. Until you can live out your message of faith, you are not yet a voice to be reckoned with. There is a world of infinite possibilities; it is the world of the Word. We need to communicate the truth of that Word to our world by the way we live our lives. Otherwise, we are just empty drums.

There was something the woman with the issue of blood knew, that was elusive to the rest of the crowd. It was simply this: all you need is an internal resolve to step out in faith and a confidence in the power of God; a deep conviction in your heart of hearts that God is able to work a miracle, despite the very real problems you are facing and the overwhelming difficulties of your situation. Yes! God can!

Many in the crowd were — and they still are today — only nuisances to the purposes of God, easily excited by every new fad and charmer in town. Often, when these people returned home, they remained the same as they were before they had seen and heard Jesus. Similarly, many who shout in public today do not even know how to whisper to Heaven in secret. It must be emphasized, however, that a good number of the men and women whom God is using in the forefront of His crusades today are people of great faith, who have a perpetual, intimate relationship with Him.

The voices of those who know how to talk to their God in secret echo stronger throughout Heaven than the loudest speaker ever created in the history of man. Their supplications attract the attention of God faster than all the noise-making of the largest public meeting. We must learn to pray at home first!

In *Luke 8:42* the writer noted that the crowd almost crushed Jesus. This unique woman was not a part of the "crush-rush". All she had was a touch capable of making a convincing difference when compared with the stampede. And Jesus commended her faith as good enough to put her biological chaos in order.

There are yet some people with such great "contact-power" today. Whenever they touch Heaven, God Himself knows they have come. He knows that someone has just got a miracle. How well can you touch God? Why touch Him casually and indifferently, when you can touch Him in faith and make a total and lasting difference? You can touch Heaven with your prayers, if you learn to pray with a deep, abiding faith in Almighty God.

The Shunammite woman would not settle for the devil's scraps. She would rather not have a boy than have one and lose him. When death laughed in her face, she knew whom to get mad at and how to find her way out of hell. In the face of adversity, she was still in control of her emotions. She did not burst into tears, screaming, "Honey! It looks like the baby is no more breathing!" She held herself together and went to the right place. She demanded to see the right person:

> "Did I ask you for a son, my lord?" she said. "Didn't I tell you, 'Don't raise my hopes'?"
>
> *2 Kings 4:28*

Whoa! There was no need to build castles in the air. If God had something for her, it had to be for real. The Shunammite woman would not budge an inch until she got God on her case. If she lived today, she would have said words like: "Look here, man of God, you started all this and now is the time to finish the job. How could you ask God to give me a miracle that would not last? You can't just send your personal assistant to my house with a bottle of oil and a handkerchief. Get down with me and finish this business before my husband hears anything of it — he is still not aware of the boy's condition and he must not be." She was so mad at the prospect of losing God's gift!

She probably could have said to the prophet, "Come quickly, otherwise I will move in with you!" When her chips were down, she was determined to go to the right place to put things right. It is high time you got the right person on the job. It is high time you sought God, and God alone. Give Him no option when it comes to restoring your joy, your health and your children. Don't settle for the scraps anymore and stop jumping around in all the wrong places.

Get positively desperate. If you can put your foot on the ground before God, He will tend to you. He will get that addiction out of that man. He will separate that child from drugs and every wrong influence. He will break those bad habits and dissolve that harmful relationship. All you need to do is to get God on the job of touching and working on their hearts.

Don't just stand there in despair while Satan does whatever he likes. Bring it on! Get God on the scene. One whisper from Heaven will do more than all your screams. Get serious with God and stay with Him until He agrees to come and see for Himself. The Shunammite woman said, "As surely as the LORD lives and as you live, I will not leave you." *So he got up and followed her (2 Kings 4:30)*. God can wipe away those tears if you insist! Most earnestly do I say to you: don't let go until He consents and does what you ask.

So the prophet Elisha got up and followed her. Gehazi, his servant, went on ahead but could not bring the boy back to life; so he gave up. You can't settle for less, like the Gehazis of this world. Most people do; they give up too easily. They would rather take the law into their own hands and see how they can fix it on their own. But unique people never give up until God grants their requests. The just *shall* live by faith. Women are said to be fragile, timid, fickle-minded and chicken-hearted. But I believe such are not the unique women we are talking about here.

Unique women are women of great and strategic faith as well as spiritual forte. They will not mind staking their all to get the one thing of great prize — as **Rahab** did. She did not care whether the Canaanite army was about to invade her home or if her country was on the verge of collapse because it was standing in God's way. All she cared about was reaching a treaty with God and enlisting on His agenda. If she could get God on her side, then Jericho could go. She told the spies: "Promise me!" (*Joshua 2: 12-13*) She wanted a better deal in life than what she had got so far; a better destiny than her lot in life thus far as a harlot — and she wanted it badly. She was a prostitute; but her past didn't count when she decided to risk her life, and all she had, to shield the Israelite spies.

There was something more important God could give her; she laid hold of a promise He had given to His people. Given half a chance to be saved, she grabbed at it with all she had. It was more important to her than all of Jericho put together. She looked like a sell-out but she was just so sold on God. How could anyone ever reject such an opportunity to be saved?

Esther was another unique woman, beautiful and without a trace of arrogance. She acknowledged God's power and understood the implications of divine purpose and appointment. Though she was a queen, she heeded the instructions of godly people older and more experienced than she was.

When the destiny of a whole nation depended on her, she insisted that they pray and fast before she made her move. She trusted, not in her own beauty and her influence over her husband the king, but in the power of God to save His people. The king was her husband but she knew it would take God to get him to grant her request. When the going got tough, she got tougher; she went ahead to risk her life in order to save ancient Israel yet again. This woman of faith was a unique lady, one who can teach us an important lesson: *that against all odds, we should go ahead and do what is right.*

She had guts. Faith never gives up on God. The unique person never gives up on God either; she is full of faith as long as she has breath. Queen Esther was the very opposite of her arrogant predecessor, Queen Vashti. She was humble, yet courageous and steadfast in her resolve to see others helped as much as she had been helped.

> Then Esther sent this reply to Mordecai: "Go, gather together all the Jews who are in Susa, and fast for me. Do not eat or drink for three days, night or day. I and my maids will fast as you do. When this is done, I will go to the king, even though it is against the law. And if I perish, I perish."
>
> *Esther 4: 15-17*

Now, I have to tell you here: don't try this until you have *prayed and fasted* first. Until these are done — *praying and fasting* — you might be making the biggest mistake of your life to break the norms of your culture or the laws of your land, such as Queen Esther did here.

"The effectual and fervent prayer of the righteous makes much power available." You won't get your breakthroughs until you have prayed through, with fasting and faith in God.

For decades, this woman has been celebrated for her statement: *"I will go to the king, even though it is against the law. And if I perish, I perish."* It seemed like she had chosen to look death straight in the eye by going against the decree of the king, her husband. However, many people who have made such similar statements in history ended up living, after all. One thing they all did was to *fast and pray* before laying their lives on the line.

Yes, there was one thing about Esther that made her unique in her day. It was what she believed when she said, "When this is done." What was it that must be done before she became a national knight in shining armor? *It was fasting and prayer!*

Until she had prayed and fasted enough, she would never have dared enter into the chamber of a despot like her own husband, King Xerxes. No! Convinced as she was that the matter must first be settled with God in the realms of the spirit, she initiated a time of fasting and prayer. She laid her hands on it in the Spirit before she made any physical move.

The unique person never goes to war with unproved weapons. Queen Esther needed to *pray and fast it out* before she made her move. Unique people are, without a doubt, men and women with great prayer lives. Some are also renowned for much fasting. Kathryn Kuhlman, for example, got so emaciated from fasting it looked like she could break down any time. Prayer helps you develop great guts! *Pray!*

Esther knew her chips weren't down yet, because it wasn't defeat she saw while she was praying and fasting. She didn't go into her husband's fortress depending on expensive cologne, make-up or attire to win favor with him. She didn't waste time painting herself when all Israel needed to be saved from genocide. At that moment her beauty didn't count. She needed to get on her knees, praying and fasting.

Though her beauty got her to be queen, it wouldn't have saved her from the king's wrath if she had walked into his court against his orders. Her beauty would not have saved any man, let alone a whole nation.

Great people are unique, they are national liberators. They are people who go all the way out to salvage the destinies of men and women alike, sons and daughters together. They don't only help their families; they help the rest of their world. Although they appreciate the advantages of looking good, they also know that there are times when the only thing that counts is not their beauty but their prayers. It is God's people praying and fasting that has helped, on many occasions, to avert national and even worldwide disasters.

With a genuine life of prayer and fasting, you can achieve great spiritual breakthroughs; you can break in on any devil and deal with every imaginable evil that comes against you; you can say to yourself and your friends, "Dying is not enough to scare me out of living and winning." It is okay to challenge death, if that is the hurdle that stands between you and life. But it can only be done with God on your side.

> They overcame him [Satan] by the blood of the Lamb and by the word of their testimony; they did not love their lives so much as to shrink from death.
>
> *Revelation 12:11*

Death does not only end life; it also serves as a gateway to life everlasting. The above passage from Revelation describes God's people who were overcomers in the face of the enemy's onslaught. They were not afraid to die for their faith; they were not cowed into silence but boldly proclaimed their belief in Christ. They discovered that the blood of Jesus shed on the cross was able to preserve them. *There is power in the blood*. They were not afraid to take the offensive in proclaiming their faith and, because of that, they made a lot of difference in the lives of people around them.

How well can you stamp your feet on the ground and say *no* to the devil's plans for you and for your spouse, children, family and country? How well can you? Most people are so educated and critical of everything, they never say *yes* to God; they keep wondering *how can?*

Faith is not "reasonable" but patient enough to rule in the world of reasonable men.

But, as for you, you can be unique; you can be the one who stands apart from the crowd and says, "I believe it when God says it, and that settles it!" You know that the *how* is not your business but God's; your business is to do your part and let God figure out the rest.

God has a plan and all He needs is someone who will agree to come on His team. Not necessarily to play for Him; He just needs someone who doesn't mind cheering and watching Him play against the enemy. We will all face death someday; but not all of us will face eternal life thereafter. Which do you choose today — life or death? Choose life by cheering on God's team now.

If you choose life, you need to live by faith; and living by faith implies daring to die for what you believe in, what you are passionate about. All things are possible with God; He is very much able to do great and wonderful things for you — and you are also able to attain all that He desires for you by His grace and power.

> Behold the handmaid of the Lord; be it unto me according to thy word.
>
> *Luke 1:38, KJV*

Are you fully prepared for something great to happen to you? **Mary** was; she was ready for all that God had for her. If being the mother of the Christ was what God wanted of her, it was okay with her! Unique people align themselves with God instead of contending with Him.

I often wonder what would have happened if Mary had not agreed to what the angel announced to her. What would have happened if she had protested when Gabriel told her she would become a mother? It *was* incredible, after all — for crying out loud, she was a virgin and she was not planning on going the family way just yet!

The "how" is not your business but God's. All you need to do is agree with Him.

She was a young lady engaged to a carpenter, Brother Joseph. She had no record of service in the temple or of holding any particular office of honor. She was neither a priestess nor a prophetess. When the angel visited her, it was probably the first time she had set her eyes on one; but she accepted his message.

Now, in contrast, consider Zechariah, the man of God. He was a serving priest. He would have had opportunities to learn about angels, and could even have seen them himself, in his long years of service in the temple. He had probably prayed to God on many occasions for a child. Yet, he doubted God's message to him when an angel visited him in the Most Holy Place while he was carrying out his priestly duties. See, he wanted a child badly but doubted that God would give him one. Outside, his congregation was fervently praying but, inside his office, he was struggling with a herald from Heaven.

Zechariah is a classic example of someone who cannot believe God for the impossible. Would you have believed and behaved differently from him? Maybe not... he was an old man and he had a wife as old as himself! What the angel told him seemed too unrealistic to happen. Yeah... but Mary's case was just as exceptional too! Actually, telling a virgin she would be pregnant wasn't just as ridiculous as telling a sterile old man his wife would be pregnant; it was much more ridiculous! Yet Mary believed. She decided to take a unique step of faith and the very thing that was impossible happened.

How many Zechariahs do we have today? How many preachers are there who still believe and apply what they preach? The ways of God may not necessarily seem logical or in accordance with man's reasoning.

Unique People

A number of people in Bible times and in our day have proven themselves to be unique. They are people who press in where others fear to tread. They dare to be different. They choose to impact their world positively. They were not born in any unique way, neither did they grow up in any unusual manner; but they decided to go up against the odds and believe God for the impossible. They walked the unique path; they walked with God. He really wants you to come along too — and it's still not too late for you to do so!

Take, for example, Mary Slessor, a Christian missionary who stopped the killing of twin babies in Africa. What do you think made women like her — and other missionaries — leave their home countries for Africa? They left the comforts and pleasures of the western world for the mosquitoes and scorching sun of Africa. The truth is that they took a bold step of faith towards their missionary vocation.

Mary Slessor dared to be different from other women of her time, and she came up doing something grand. She stemmed the killing of twin babies. Prior to her arrival in Africa, that was a traditional practice which had its origins in the superstitious beliefs held by African tribes.

A unique woman, you will agree? Maybe she would have done something else back home if she had not gone out to Africa — but it might not be anything as wonderful as giving all those babies a chance to live. Twins are such amazing creations of God and — thanks to a Christian missionary — those in Africa had their chance to live a full life.

A Unique God

What more can be said? It doesn't take much to understand this concept of uniqueness, for our God is a unique God too. The Scriptures record:

> But God hath chosen the foolish things of the world to confound the wise; and God hath chosen the weak things of the world to confound the things which are mighty; and base things of the world, and things which are despised, hath God chosen, yea, and things which are not, to bring to nought things that are.
>
> *1 Corinthians 1: 27-28, KJV*

Envisage that! God delights in driving so-called wise people crazy with what might be considered lowly, little and laughable. The world today is traumatized by all the violence unleashed by the wicked. Some in various parts of the great Arab empire have sold out to a war of eliminating every non-conformist to their *faith*. And the rest of the world is set on edge simply because there is a group of people whose ideology subscribes to the idea that the "good works" acceptable to their god include *killing "unbelievers" for him!*

But our God is not a terrorist or coward who wastes the lives of His children in a campaign for primacy against so-called "infidels". Whether you believe or deny Him, He doesn't have to harm or kill anyone to prove His existence or preeminence. It is definitely amazing that God is so longsuffering towards the worst of men. The very idea of killing for our God is anathema to a true believer in God.

Some people really need to understand the meaning of the three-lettered word *GOD* — just so that they can be cured of the grievous psychopathic tendencies they demonstrate towards humankind. It is acceptable in the archives of human history to fight for one's own personal interests, rights and privileges. But what is a man trying to say when he sets out on a "holy war" to defend his god and to protect his god's interests, at the expense of his own life and that of his fellowmen?

"If Baal is god, let him fight for himself." That's what Joash said to the Israelites who demanded that his son Gideon be put to death for desecrating their idol's altar.

> But Joash replied to the hostile crowd around him, "Are you going to plead Baal's cause? Are you trying to save him? Whoever fights for him shall be put to death by morning! If Baal really is a god, he can defend himself when someone breaks down his altar."
>
> *Judges 6:31*

We don't fight for God. Instead, He fights for us — what a unique God! Start minding your own business and let God mind His. Yours is to worship Him while His is to fight for you and Himself if need be. He said to wise and righteous Brother Job:

> "Will the one who contends with the Almighty correct him? Let him who accuses God answer him!"
>
> *Job 40:2*

Then Job answered the LORD:

> "I am unworthy — how can I reply to you? I put my hand over my mouth. I spoke once, but I have no answer — twice, but I will say no more."
>
> *Job 40: 4-5*

And God answered Job out of the storm:

> "Brace yourself like a man; I will question you, and you shall answer me."
>
> *Job 38:3, 40:7*

> "Can you pull in the leviathan with a fishhook or tie down his tongue with a rope?"
>
> *Job 41:1*

As far as God was concerned, Brother Job talked and boasted too much. *Do you?* When it came to jousting with God, he was not up to the mark. And, after failing twice to give a smart answer to God's questions, he decided he had better shut his mouth with his hand.

The leviathan was an enormous, multiple-headed sea creature that God invited Job to try his skills on — but he knew better than to do that! In *Psalm 74:14* we learn that God was the one who defeated the Leviathan and gave it away as food to the desert dwellers: *It was you who crushed the heads of Leviathan and gave him as food to the creatures of the desert* (NIV). The King James Version says:

> Thou brakest the heads of leviathan in pieces, and gavest him to be meat to the people inhabiting the wilderness.
>
> *Psalm 74:14, KJV*

Water is very rarely found in the desert or wilderness; these are not places close to water. Yet God can break the heads of leviathan, a huge creature found only in mighty waters, and feed its meat to remote desert dwellers, to their full satisfaction! What a great God!

You can negotiate the colors of your future with what you ask for with your mouth today.

Sometimes you don't have to be anywhere near the resources you need for God to supply your needs. Desert dwellers don't go fishing but with God they can enjoy the fattest of the fatness ordinarily found in mighty waters. What the wisdom of man cannot accomplish — even when given all the resources needed — the wisdom of God will accomplish with no resources in sight. You can bet He is a unique God. He said:

> "For my thoughts are not your thoughts, neither are your ways my ways," declares the LORD.
> "As the heavens are higher than the earth, so are my ways higher than your ways and my thoughts than your thoughts."
>
> *Isaiah 55: 8-9*

His thoughts and His ways are different from those of the world, and He calls us to be like Him: not thinking or acting like the world does, but to be a unique people separated unto Him — as Deborah, Esther, Mary Magdalene, Rahab, Mary the mother of Christ, and others have been in their time. You too can be, in this time!

CHAPTER 5

One Woman's Way of Winning

Industrious, Honorable, Kind and Respectful

God's Side Always Wins

> Then Deborah said to Barak, "Go! This is the day the LORD has given Sisera into your hands. Has not the LORD gone ahead of you?" So Barak went down Mount Tabor, followed by ten thousand men.
>
> At Barak's advance, the LORD routed Sisera and all his chariots and army by sword, and Sisera abandoned his chariot and fled on foot. But Barak pursued the chariots and army as far as Harosheth Haggoyim. All the troops of Sisera fell by the sword; not a man was left.
>
> *Judges 4: 14-16*

It is only God who can bring powerful oppressors to their knees — which is why we must ensure that we have God's instructions and strategies before we take on the enemy. In spite of the distress we may be suffering, we must wait on God until He gives us the go-ahead to act.

Until God commanded them to advance against Jabin and Sisera, Israel did not go to war. The best way to defeat the wicked is by following divine instructions. Any other way will be a mere waste of precious resources. God still goes to war; He still commands a strike force — but on His own terms, in His own time, and by His own strategies.

Definitely, when God comes on your side, the toughest of adversaries will have no other choice but to take to their heels. When God is at work with you, your adversaries will be put to flight. Your greatest fear becomes your greatest victory when God is in charge. All of Israel went to war against the iron man Sisera, not out of desperation but because they were convinced they would win.

> Sisera, however, fled on foot to the tent of Jael, the wife of Heber the Kenite, because there were friendly relations between Jabin king of Hazor and the clan of Heber the Kenite.
>
> *Judges 4:17*

The record states: *"Sisera, however, fled."* This flight was against Sisera's wishes and, if he had his own way, he would have stayed for the fight. But, this time, God scared him so badly that he ran for his dear life barefooted. This is what will happen to your adversary when God takes sides with you — and now is the time to bring Him on board.

What will set your adversaries on the run? It is the sight of you at war *on God's terms*. When the tide of God turns against your adversaries, they become the prey of those they have oppressed and preyed upon. However, it is only the God of heaven and earth who can make cowards out of despots; it is not right for any man to boast of such a feat. What can you do on your own?

Honor for a Fearful Commander

> Sisera, however, *fled on foot* to the tent of Jael, the wife of Heber the Kenite, because there were friendly relations between Jabin King of Hazor and the clan of Heber the Kenite. Jael went out to meet Sisera and said to him, "Come, my lord, come right in. Don't be afraid." So he entered her tent, and she put a covering over him.
>
> *Judges 4: 17-18*

Sisera fled on foot to Jael's tent. How else would you recognize a defeated soldier but by his feet? Sisera didn't have his boots on. He ran barefooted. Upon his arrival at her residence, however, Jael did not ridicule this man; instead, she honored him by calling him "my lord". This is a salutation used by ancient Jewish women when referring to their husbands or other venerable persons.

Sisera was the strongman who held Israel in his cruel grip until God devised his doom. Up to this time, everyone had feared him, for he was the commander of

Doing what people mind doing gets you results people don't mind getting.

King Jabin's ruthless army; but, when God's own army showed up, this same Sisera was thoroughly overwhelmed. He ran for his dear life, barefooted. On his way he met a lady with great etiquette who, barefooted as he was, nonetheless showed him respect — and that was the last straw that broke the camel's back. When you accord people respect, you will gain their confidence, and they will get comfortable around you. Rare opportunities come to you when folks are comfortable with and around you.

Jael did an unusual thing: she did not wait for Sisera to ask for help but offered it to him at once. She knew his desire was for refuge, a place to hide — and in her tent, to be precise. So, before he even asked, she was already inviting him in: *Jael went out to meet Sisera and said to him, "Come, my lord, come right in."* When you learn to be helpful, you will discover that you have the energy to mobilize power and influence around you. Jael could not wait to exterminate a wicked regime; she took in its strongman at once.

Despite the fact that Sisera had lost his place and power, Jael still honored him — at least to get a good job done.

Honor Others — and God Will Honor You

Some folks are not useful to God simply because of their wrong attitude; their arrogance is their undoing. This is so because, even when opportunities for success come their way, their haughty airs make victory elusive. Arrogance and insolence don't really look good on anyone. They only cheat you out of your privileges. Unlike those arrogant folks, there are others who find favor with God and man because they treat everyone with honor and respect. These are the people who receive great privileges from God, even though they may be battling tremendous odds in life.

One of the requirements of spiritual governance is order. There are hierarchies in the spirit realm and, though Satan is a fallen angel, God's archangel Michael did not insult him during a dispute.

> But even the archangel Michael, when he was disputing with the devil about the body of Moses, did not dare to bring a slanderous accusation against him, but said, "The LORD rebuke you!"
>
> *Jude 9*

Another example of spiritual order can be found in *Daniel 10: 12-14*. A messenger angel had been sent from heaven in response to Daniel's prayers. But, while this angel was on his way to Daniel, he was held hostage by the "Prince of Persia" (a demon who exercised influence over the Persian realm). It took the great archangel Michael to free the messenger angel so that he could go to Daniel. The point is, while he was being detained, the angel did not start yelling at the fallen "Prince of Persia"; he did not behave rudely towards this demon who had once been a high-ranking angel.

Jael understood this concept of following a proper order in fulfilling God's purposes. You won't be given a position of authority if you refuse to learn and apply even the rudiments of common courtesy. Do not speak arrogantly. Do not talk to people disrespectfully. Do not behave in an offensive manner towards others. King Rehoboam, in his arrogance, rejected the counsel of the elders of his time and took the advice of his pals. He spoke offensively to the Israelites. The result was that many in Israel rebelled against him and his kingdom became divided. (*2 Chronicles 10: 1-19*)

Now, compare him with Esther, another beautiful lady who knew how to treat people with respect. During her growing-up years she took care to obey her guardian, Mordecai. She carried this attitude of honoring her elders with her when she got into the Persian king's harem. Unlike the other smart-aleck candidates, who thought they knew better and did whatever they deemed fit when they appeared before King Xerxes, Esther acted on the advice of Hegai, the king's eunuch who was in charge of the harem. As a result, she won the king's favor and approval more than the other ladies, and was made Queen. (*Esther 2: 5-18*)

Respect for others, however, does not mean submitting blindly to their dictates. There are times when one has to break the rules to save lives or fight against injustice. Queen Esther showed her mettle some years later, when the evil Haman plotted to exterminate the Jews in Xerxes' kingdom. The only way they could be saved was for her to appeal to the king on their behalf — a bold act that could have gotten her executed, as death was the punishment for anyone who dared enter Xerxes' presence uninvited by him. Esther, however, kept her head and held onto her manners even in the midst of turmoil and impending danger.

First, she got all the Jews to fast and pray, and she did likewise. Then, she put her life on the line by appearing unasked before the king. But — and this is important — she didn't rush brashly into his presence. She showed the utmost respect for Xerxes and thereby gained his favor. This led ultimately to the triumph of the Jews and the execution of their enemy, Haman.

When we choose to act rudely, we evoke a similar response from others — and then in turn we tend to retaliate in like manner. This will only escalate into absolute chaos and unimaginable horror as the hatred continues to intensify. The world needs people who can bring order out of such chaos; people who can pour oil on troubled waters.

There was war in the region and an enemy was in flight — fleeing, probably so that he could reconsolidate his power and return to make more trouble another day. Yet here was this woman, Jael, who could calm strained nerves and keep her head and her good manners in the midst of the mess and chaos.

Maybe if Jael had added her voice to the revolutionary ranting, Sisera would have thought twice before putting up at her apartment. We cannot fight the vulgar with vulgarities as that leave us not much different from our foes. There might be revolutions here and there, but there are no fighters as powerful and effective as an evolutionary force.

A truly evolutionary force is tender, thorough and tutored. These are people who remain calm and collected in the face of adversity. They bless folks who curse them and give shelter to those who ostracize them. Their attitude in the long run goes to prove that vengeance is God's and, when He is set to turn the tables against wickedness, it will not be in a chaotic but strategic way. Still waters run deep where shallow waters are prone to spew out agitations.

Refuge for a Fleeing Commander-in-Chief

Jael went out to meet Sisera and said to him, "Come, my lord, come right in. Don't be afraid." So he entered her tent, and she put a covering over him.

"I'm thirsty," he said. "Please give me some water." She opened a skin of milk, gave him a drink, and covered him up.

"Stand in the doorway of the tent," he told her. "If someone comes by and asks you, 'Is anyone here?' say 'No.'"

But Jael, Heber's wife, picked up a tent peg and a hammer and went quietly to him while he lay fast asleep, exhausted. She drove the peg through his temple into the ground, and he died.

Barak came by in pursuit of Sisera, and Jael went out to meet him. "Come," she said, "I will show you the man you're looking for." So he went in with her, and there lay Sisera with the tent peg through his temple — dead.

On that day God subdued Jabin, the Canaanite king, before the Israelites. And the hand of the Israelites grew stronger and stronger against Jabin, the Canaanite king, until they destroyed him.

Judges 4: 18-24

Jael was at home when Israel went to war against Sisera and his army. She did not go to war but the victory came to her because she was the one who eventually determined where the buck stopped, by the power of a smart attitude. A truly unique person does not pass the buck. If you *will* be unique, you *won't* support wrongdoing; you *won't* fold your hands and cross your legs and watch with impunity as mischief dances along, passing you by; you *will* stop the surge of evil wherever you meet it. *Don't be afraid to let your world know where you stand on this.*

Before the war started, Barak had given away the credit for his conquest to a woman; but it did not go to an ordinary one. It went to a unique woman who was worthy of it.

Barak said to [Deborah], "If you go with me, I will go; but if you don't go with me, I won't go."

"Very well," Deborah said, "I will go with you. But because of the way you are going about this, the honor will not be yours, for **the LORD will hand Sisera over to a woman.**" So Deborah went with Barak to Kedesh.

Judges 4: 8-9

Now, it was not a question of whether the battle would end in success or not; it was a question of *who* was willing to be the champion in pursuit of victory — and that willing person was Jael, right there in her own home and not on the battlefield. It could have been anybody, but she was the one who availed herself of the privilege.

*Sisera... fled on foot to the tent of Jael, the wife of Heber the Kenite... **Jael went out to meet Sisera** and said to him, "Come, my lord, come right in. Don't be afraid."*

Victory comes only to people who *will* rightly work and go for it. We can't just sit around at home and expect success to fall into our laps. We must go out and invest in life positively and resourcefully. We must take some form of action, be it learning a trade, studying a course, starting an enterprise, meeting people, or working hard to acquire resources that will enable us to achieve our goals.

Although Jael was a wife and a woman in a male-centric society, she had an estate she could call her own. Tents were used for lodging in Deborah's days and Jael must have worked hard to either acquire or keep one for herself. Whatever resources you have worked hard to acquire will go a long way to give you an edge in your endeavors; it will enhance your chances in life.

Sisera asked for water but she gave him milk. She gave him better than what he asked for. She must have been a woman who could contain her feelings well and show a good attitude. If you are highly expressive, it is important that you learn how to manage your emotions. All the while Jael was getting the milk, nothing about her countenance betrayed her agenda — not even to a shrewd military commander like Sisera. He was no fool; his many years on the battlefield would have honed his instincts for danger. But Jael outwitted him with her wisdom, cool head and calm demeanor.

She had her wits about her; calm and collected she stood in front of her tent, eyeing the runaway warrior. What were the thoughts that went through her mind? We can only imagine. Nevertheless she did not meet Sisera, screaming: *"Yes, today is your doomsday! You Wicked Man, you don't even deserve to live and, if you dare come into my tent, I'll call the Police!"* Whatever she was thinking, it was a friendly, sympathetic face that she showed to the fugitive.

She knew how to trap a tyrant on the run. It is not by senseless ranting. She was relaxed, yet at war. She was God's chosen instrument to put an end to the cruel oppression of ancient Israel.

Your chances of survival are high when you bite the bullet of a foe and slim when you run from a barking dog.

What made her the right person for this honor? Following from what we have said earlier, three key reasons were: one, she had an available place of refuge, her tent; two, she could manage her emotions well and show proper courtesy even to her enemy; and, three, she was a very brave and resourceful woman.

The best way of defeating a stronger adversary is to wait until he gets exhausted before you assail him. Jael was a cut above other women in her day. She was the wife of Heber, who was most likely the chief of the Kenite clan. So she was also an influential and informed person in her own right. She had resources of her own; she had her own tent — just as Deborah had her own palm tree.

There were other places Sisera could have gone to for solace but he chose Jael's tent. It must have been a huge and cozy — perhaps even a luxurious — place, for it would have been beneath Sisera to hide in a tiny hole. It takes an enterprising woman to acquire such a tent as well as enough resources of her own to host a "big military buff" like Sisera. And, without those resources, she would not have had the privilege of luring the tyrant to his death.

This is what you must do: endeavor as much as possible to be a successful person because success has many friends but failure is a very lonely orphan. Success grants you great privileges and opportunities to stop the spread of wickedness.

It is very difficult to fight the evil and corruption rampant in high places when you only exist at the grassroots level. And, as long as the bourgeoisie are the ones sponsoring wickedness, the proletariat will have little power against it! Corrupt nations need successful and ingenious people like Jael in the corridors of power so as to secure their destinies, keep them from being eaten up by impiety, and ensure that wickedness is brought to book. Until then, noises of protest may continue on the streets but nobody will care enough to do anything about the wrongs that need to be corrected.

Thanks to Jael; but for her, Sisera could have escaped to some safe haven or place of refuge before Barak could do anything about him. And I keep wondering what would have happened to ancient Israel back in the days of King Xerxes of Persia, if Esther had not been the wife of this king. Both women were timely miracles who came up trumps to save their people.

This is a simple but bitter truth: the common man or woman on the street or in the marketplace can do little — and sometimes absolutely nothing — to influence the most crucial events that cause the greatest impact on society. Godly people must seek to rise to positions of power and influence, and take a stand for righteousness when they are at the top of the hierarchy; this is a responsibility that we owe to ourselves and that we must strive to fulfill.

We can't send God on errands He has delegated to us. If we refuse to touch the system, God has no point of impact. We must get involved as much as possible! We must cast our votes on the side of godliness and make them count while we can.

If you don't settle for the "small", you will get the "big".

If Jael were not the wife of Heber and if she did not have a tent wherein Sisera could seek refuge, she would not have had the privilege of delivering the Israelites from their oppressor. The world needs successful and righteous people who abhor evil and will fight to bring down tyranny and corruption in high places. They are needed as politicians and as companions to government officials. This is one obvious way godly people can win.

Milk for a Thirsty General

> So he entered her tent, and she put a covering over him.
>
> **"I'm thirsty,"** he said. "Please **give me some water." She opened a skin of milk, gave him a drink,** and covered him up.
>
> "Stand in the doorway of the tent," he told her. "If someone comes by and asks you, 'Is anyone here?' say 'No.'"
>
> *Judges 4: 18-20*

Here, he was teaching her to lie to protect him, but little did he know that he would die in her tent; that his nemesis would not come from without but from within his place of refuge. I have wondered at times: what sort of a woman was Jael? She seemed to have gone about exterminating the enemy as though she were a trained assassin. Perhaps she was only an instrument in God's hands, for He is the one who sets traps for the wicked:

> Be sure of this: The wicked will not go unpunished, but those who are righteous will go free.
>
> *Proverbs 11:21*

> But the Lord laughs at the wicked, for he knows their day is coming …their swords will pierce their own hearts, and their bows will be broken.
>
> *Psalm 37: 13, 15*

This wicked man asked only for water and, when he got milk, he was not smart enough to suspect foul play. Because God was against him, Sisera in his extreme exhaustion lost all sense of danger. Milk in the place of water is certainly an exceptional way of terminating the life of a ruthless and evil man. She went out of her way to give him milk when all he asked for was water. She was the stronger, for she possessed the most subtle yet most lethal weapon of war: kindness; the kind act of offering milk to one's enemy. *Milk signifies kindness.*

"You have heard that it was said, 'Love your neighbor and hate your enemy.' But I tell you: Love your enemies and pray for those who persecute you, that you may be sons of your Father in heaven."

Matthew 5: 43-45

Prior to this moment, she must have held serious grudges against this man who had taken refuge in her tent, although her husband was his acquaintance. So she brought his fearful soul into her tent and there she nurtured him to death. She was very kind to him all the way, so much so that when all he asked for was water, she gave him milk. She also covered him up, although her intention was to eradicate him in the end. She was so good to him; he had to die paying for that kindness. What a deal of kindness and what a woman!

When God is all set to bring judgment on wickedness, one thing He will surely do: He will definitely grant the wicked folks comfort in the place of doom — or how else do we explain Sisera's misfortune? I am trying to imagine what must have been going on in Jael's mind all the while when she was being nice to her prey.

She knew she would definitely lose if she took on Sisera in a one-to-one tussle. She was a woman and he was a soldier. She was obviously not on her way to the gym when Sisera came by. He was a man with vigorous muscles, having just escaped from the warfront. Hence, Sisera was obviously the favored contender if it came to a hand-to-hand tussle between a military General and a civilian woman. Thus, it was actually wiser for Jael not to attack him until he was totally exhausted.

Today, many have made expensive mistakes and may still live to regret them — mistakes such as challenging an enemy when he is in better form or has the better advantage.

If we choose to plunge headlong and recklessly into the battles of life, we will end up losing and nursing our wounds. If we fight our enemies with their own weapons, we will be playing a losing game. Our style of warfare should not be the one commonly used by the world.

> Wisdom is better than weapons of war, but one sinner destroys much good.
>
> *Ecclesiastes 9:18*

> In truthful speech and in the power of God; with weapons of righteousness in the right hand and in the left...
>
> *2 Corinthians 6:7*

> The weapons we fight with are not the weapons of the world. On the contrary, they have divine power to demolish strongholds.
>
> *2 Corinthians 10:4*

To live in prosperity and still be able to retain an attitude of courtesy and respect towards others, and be as kind as possible to them: such behavior releases highly exceptional power from heaven. This power is very unlike that wielded by unbelieving and cruel folk. The affluence of the ungodly eventually leads to rottenness in their bones, and the generations after them are suddenly cut off, no longer to be of any reckoning; whereas the affluence of the godly is imparted from generation to generation. This is so, simply because most wealthy folk who are wicked are prone to be disrespectful and unkind — and what they give unto others eventually goes back to them.

Hence, acting foolishly is an expensive mistake in spiritual matters. Jael understood that there are some battles you do not fight head-on. You must wait till you have a better advantage. Many believers go about their lives following common and everyday human strategies. They want to do the impossible by beating the world at its own game. Many of us claim to be "born again" but we want to have our cake and eat it too. You claim to be godly, yet there are still some things about you that look quite ungodly. If you are true to your faith, what then is the meaning of the offence you continue to perpetrate?

Today, I see believers who want to play along with the world, all in the name of gaining the world for God. We want to follow the pattern of the world, talking, walking and working the way everyone else does. The pathetic truth is that our attempts to reach the world in a noxious manner have resulted instead in the world encroaching on our faith. We are losing more ground through our compromises than we are able to gain. We are losing much of our credibility through our imprudence in compromising the fundamental principles of our Christian faith.

We can't change the world by employing malevolent strategies. We can't inspire faith by singing the same types of songs as the world does. We can't enlighten peoples' darkness as long as preachers parade around like they are no more than mere motivational speakers, even making affluent infidels their reference points in a vain bid to prove that God wants man to prosper.

Why should we draw our examples from the world? Oh! What foolishness! A preacher, after trying hard, succeeded in inviting a philosopher to his church and then made the great mistake of philosophizing from the pulpit whilst presenting his sermon. At the end of the service, while he was still feeling great about himself, the philosopher walked up to him and said, *"Sir, why don't you stick to your Bible and allow philosophers to preach philosophy? As matter of fact, all you said today was elementary philosophy."* That's the most embarrassing remark anyone can hear about himself!

Carl FH Henry realized that the "new evangelical" appeal of the late 1940s, for Christians to infiltrate society, had sadly been accompanied by an unfortunate development. An excruciatingly large number of evangelicals had been impacted by the secular values of the culture they were trying to reach for Christ. He alleged that, while evangelicals sought to make a way into the culture, the culture concurrently made bewildering inroads into evangelical life. A distressing number of church folks now cling to the idols of money, material possessions, sex and the status-quo: all those idols which are now bewitching the modern world.

Today, many believers are stepping to the rhythm of the world; but we cannot play ball like the rest of the world and still expect to win. We need to start fighting our battles God's way. We need to stop preaching psychology and philosophy in the church. We don't need motivational speakers in the pulpit. All we need are the bearers of the light and the lovers of God: the custodians of the truth and power of God.

Jael understood this one principle: if our faith is to triumph against evil, then we must drive evil to the place where we can gain a better advantage over it. This is the place where the true heroes of faith have nurtured wickedness to death. This is the place of absolute obedience in compliance with divine standards. It is the place where we are strong and the adversary is weak. This was why Jael gave herself enough time to lay out her trap for Sisera. We are the children of the covenant, and we are responsible for our own complete obedience to the covenant.

And we will be ready to punish every act of disobedience, once your obedience is complete.

2 Corinthians 10:6

We are not poised to win until we reject the least iota of compromise. Total obedience to the ways of God results in the manifestation of His presence in our lives and His judgment on our disobedient enemies. This is the only place where we can gain strength against our adversaries. The better advantage we gain relies on the manifest presence of God, which is a function of our absolute commitment to His agenda.

The problems prevalent in contemporary society may well be the same as those plaguing what we call the "church" today — a church that is full of and continues to condone liars, and where preachers won't tell sinners the truth about their sins but will continue to receive the offerings of the wicked. They receive tithes and offerings from people who steal from their employers and from their nation.

We have deceived ourselves too long, thinking God's ways will not suffice until we have added a little compromise to it. God does not believe in lukewarm people. It is either you are hot or cold, faithful or unfaithful. *You can't sit on the fence in God's kingdom; it is a city without walls. You are either in or out.* You can't be neutral; you are either totally committed to Him or you are not committed to Him at all.

Jael nurtured the ruthless and wicked to death, maybe not for love but in fulfillment of prophecy. She received the medal for her victory. Her instruments of warfare were uncommon; she employed the bizarre weapons of courtesy, kindness, hospitality and right attitudes, which are only common among truly obedient believers.

These weapons of warfare are not common in the world. They look very much different from all the weapons employed by any army or terrorist group in this world. They are physically intangible but spiritually and physically effective. And, because these weapons are spiritual, they are much more lethal than any weapon humans can fashion.

Consider These

Never be lacking in zeal, but keep your spiritual fervor, serving the Lord. Be joyful in hope, **patient in affliction**, faithful in prayer. Share with God's people who are in need. **Practice hospitality**.

Romans 12: 11-13

Finally, be strong in the Lord and in his mighty power. Put on the full armor of God so that you can take your stand against the devil's schemes. For our struggle is not against flesh and blood, but against the rulers, against the authorities,   against the powers of this dark world and against   the spiritual forces of evil in the heavenly realms.

Therefore put on the full armor of God, so that when the day of evil comes, you may be able to stand your ground, and after you have done everything, to stand. Stand firm then, with the belt of truth buckled around your waist, with the breastplate of righteousness in place, and with your feet fitted with the readiness that comes from the gospel of peace. In addition to all this, take up the shield of faith, with which you can extinguish all the flaming arrows of the evil one. Take the helmet of salvation and the sword of the Spirit, which is the word of God. And pray in the Spirit on all occasions… be alert and always keep on praying for all the saints.

Ephesians 6: 10-18

CHAPTER 6

A Hungry Dog

Any dog that understands its place, rights and
privileges will reign over children who lack
kingdom understanding in such matters.

A Canaanite Woman from the Vicinity

Leaving that place, Jesus withdrew to the region of Tyre and
Sidon. A Canaanite woman from that vicinity came to him,
crying out, "Lord, Son of David, have mercy on me! My
daughter is suffering terribly from demon-possession."

Jesus did not answer a word. So his disciples came to him
and urged him, "Send her away, for she keeps crying out after
us."

He answered, "I was sent only to the lost sheep of Israel."

The woman came and knelt before him. "Lord, help me!"
she said.

He replied, "It is not right to take the children's bread and
toss it to their dogs."

"Yes Lord," she said, "but even the dogs eat the crumbs
that fall from their masters' table."

Then Jesus answered, "Woman, you have great faith! Your
request is granted."

And her daughter was healed from that very hour.

Matthew 15: 21-28

Now, you don't have to be on God's "favorites" list
(hypothetically speaking, of course; as if there were any such
favoritism, to begin with!) to cash in on His promises.
Neither do you need to be from an elite class before you can

break into the miraculous. Regardless of your background, all you need to gain access to the best in life is to be someone out there — *someone in the vicinity.*

Scripture called the mother in the above passage "a Canaanite woman from that vicinity" — a "nobody", to be precise! She was so insignificant no one knew her name, her family background, or anything else that could uniquely distinguish her. And no one even bothered to ask, after all was said and done. All we know about her is that she was not born an Israelite — in other words, by the class distinctions of that time, she was not from the upper echelons of society. She was just one of the many unknown persons out there on the streets of Tyre and Sidon. Definitely a nonentity; nonetheless she came calling on Jesus when she needed a miracle for her daughter.

She did not have a chauffeur to bring her to the conference in a Cadillac or a Limo; yet she came to the meeting. After all, it was an inclusive occasion not specially meant for a select few. So, what more would she be waiting for? And likewise, what more could we be waiting for, before we will begin to operate in the realities of God?

No one has to wait till they have earned a VIP tag before gaining access to the best there is in life. You do not have to wait for some other "right time" when a unique opportunity comes knocking on your door. At such times as these, all you need to do is simply to get down to brass tacks!

God is no respecter of persons. He is not swayed by our considerations of time. He does not take into account how clever, successful, rich or good-looking we are. He only looks down on the proud of heart. If we ignore the opportunity that presents itself today and insist on waiting for some other "right time," it may never come.

This part of my book is all about availing yourself of opportunities that beckon right in your face; creating a time to meet God when there seems to be no time at all.

So many folks live life on the sidelines because they keep making excuses for the chaos in their lives, for their short-comings, for everything and anything. If you were not born into the privileged class, it is not reason enough for you to remain downtrodden. The responsibility for initiating the responses we get from life is first and foremost ours.

Anyone who has the courage to sow a seed has the right to reap a harvest of crops, as a matter of course. And anyone who has the guts to ask purposefully has the right to receive a response. God has created everyone with the

Yet another powerful way of winning arises from one's ability to bring about order in the midst of muddle.

potential to accomplish great deeds; all we need is to "just do it". Your car has the ability to take you places but, until you turn on the ignition, nothing is going to work.

There are various ways of breaking out of stagnation and setting our lives in motion towards the things that really count. And, as long as this life remains God's show, everybody is invited to come along. Whatever your background, you can make it as long as you have signed up for it. There are no social strata in God's world but it is up to us what we make of it; for all will die but not all will have lived — truly lived. You can be one of those who have made up their minds to truly live their lives well; for every bit of life offers opportunities you can either receive or reject. The choice is entirely yours.

Mercy and Worship

When this Canaanite woman came, the first thing she asked for was mercy. There are so many self-righteous and arrogant people in today's world. They all have one thing in common: they don't excel in doing business with God. To them the idea of living on divine mercy is worthless. Instead, and by implication, they declare: "God is righteous, so are we, and there is nothing to be gained by living in dependence on Him."

This Canaanite woman, however, was sharp — very sharp — in the way she appealed for help. It is impossible to outsmart God but astute people don't lag behind Him. They always keep the right pace.

The question is: what favor can a man receive from God without His mercy? She knew her background was not such that would grant her God's favor for what she was seeking. Hence she designed a wise approach: she asked for mercy first. Mercy... Oh mercy, God's mercy! What can be more important than it? I keep wondering how she came to know this vital secret to gaining access to heaven's blessings — the one thing needed for anyone to receive God's blessings.

Secondly, she called Jesus "Lord". That was a precarious thing for her to do, going by the standards of her generation. She was a Canaanite and He was a Jew. In the context of that place and time, it amounted to treason on her part — such was the contempt that existed between the Jewish nation and its neighbors. However — either because of what she so badly needed from Him or because she understood something about Him that, even among the Jews themselves, only a few really did — she was far ahead of her time in acknowledging Jesus as her Lord.

To most Jews in His day, Jesus was no more than a carpenter's son and just another fanatic down the street; but to this woman He was Lord and He deserved her worship. Similarly too, many believers even today do not know the worth of the Man at the heart of their professed faith.

In her day, this woman would be classified as an illegitimate worshiper; however she was in fact perfectly legitimate in God's eyes. Before she ever came to worship, she had already asked for mercy. Understanding the place of mercy and worship in God's scheme of things is exceptionally important. God does not give us any blessing without our first availing ourselves of His mercy.

> "Woe to you, teachers of the law and Pharisees, you hypocrites! You give a tenth of your spices — mint, dill and cummin. But you have neglected the more important matters of the law — justice, **mercy** and faithfulness."
>
> *Matthew 23:23*

> But my **mercy** shall not depart away from him, as I took it from Saul, whom I put away before thee.
>
> *2 Samuel 7:15, KJV*

Mercy is an important aspect of God's way of dealing with man. When any man runs out of it, he gets discarded. King Saul's greatest undoing was the departure of God's mercies from him. He had his shortcomings but so did others like his successor King David.

David committed adultery with Bathsheba and went on to kill her husband, Uriah — in spite of Uriah being so unwaveringly loyal to him and so much more devoted than he was to God's Ark of covenant at that time. Yet, God did not disown David for all he had done; instead He called him a man after His own heart, and King David continued to enjoy God's mercy despite all his failures.

The only thing that can prevail against God's wrath is His mercy. With His mercy, you are divinely insured against rejection.

If you are wondering why Jesus did not tell this woman to stop following Him, although He was reluctant to attend to her, it was because she struck the chords of His mercy. She played a note God could not resist.

> And he said, LORD God of Israel, there is no God like thee, in heaven above, or on earth beneath, who keepest covenant and mercy with thy servants that walk before thee with all their heart.
>
> *1 Kings 8:23, KJV*

> And the LORD said, "I will cause all my goodness to pass in front of you, and I will proclaim my name, the LORD, in your presence. I will have mercy on whom I will have mercy, and I will have compassion on whom I will have compassion."
>
> *Exodus 33:19*

If God decides not to help a man, all that man's efforts will be in vain. He will always be incapacitated. The whole world might come to his aid but nothing will avail. If, on the other hand, God decides to help him, there is no opposition — however formidable — that can stand in the way. If you have God's mercy, you have the greatest guarantee against the odds of life!

An example of God's sovereignty in deciding whether to extend mercy to us can be drawn from His reason for saving the world. He did not decide to save humankind because we sent a "Save Our Souls" delegation to Him. The decision was His personal resolution and, though we ridiculed Him when He made the offer, He would not change His mind about it. While we were yet sinners, Jesus Christ died for us. While we were still horrible to Him, He loved us.

As dead men can't ask to live again, it is all by the mercy of God. We were dead in sin and we did not know it; yet He chose to bring us life. We were lost and we did not even know it; but His grace came searching for us. No wonder Jesus prayed that His father would forgive us when He was being crucified. Whenever Death contends with Life for the soul of a man, what is needed is Mercy. When Mercy says "No" to Death, all of Hell has to stand down — and the dying gets to live again. This is why God's Salvation is indeed His Amazing Grace.

If God were to be against you, what can you do? No mortal or spirit can take legal action against Him. He makes all His decisions single-handedly. He is not dependent on anyone's good works. A whole lot of "good" people will definitely perish because they fail to understand these dynamics of God's mercy. And you will find a whole lot of

Kindness and tenderness are lethal weapons designed to defeat wickedness. So, be nice to your foe!

seemingly bad people in Heaven because they enjoyed the benefits of God's mercy. This is a great mystery and miracle of God. Your efforts are rendered futile when God says "No". But when God says "Yes", you are blessed and, if need be, the whole world will come to your aid; your enemies will become your benefactors and people you don't even know will give generously to your cause. Mercy is so powerful. It is the one phenomenon that prevails over judgment.

For Real

After the Canaanite woman had worshipped God in her own way and after she had obtained mercy, she told the Lord her problem. She could not cover it up anymore. She did not play down her difficulties. She presented it to Jesus the way it was, for real. Her daughter was suffering — not slightly but terribly — from the devil's torments. She needed urgent help. What a predicament she was in! But we can cheer up because that's why Jesus came, and she was already having her once-in-a-lifetime audience with Him.

Some people try to cover up whatever they are going through. They paint a rosy picture of their life when they are actually going through hell and floundering in a big mess. Miracles might not come the way of such people because of their hypocrisy. We can't be insincere with God and others, and expect to be helped. A sincere heart is of great worth. It will introduce you to a miracle.

The people who go far with God are those who are open and honest with Him. They tell it the way it really is. We can tell God what we are going through, any day and any time. No problem is ever too big for Him, no trouble too much for Him to handle. He really cares to know how it is with us — though we can't hide anything from Him, anyway. Yet He might not help, however, if we aren't real with Him.

Looking around the world, I have great compassion for people who choose to live on in their pain, pretending to themselves, God and others that all is well with them when the opposite is the case. This is not about having a pity-party but about being able to accept that there is a problem and being open about it.

This woman came all the way from her home to open up to Jesus.
No one has to perish in silence. You don't have to die suffering. Say
something. Speak up! God wants to hear from you.

There is no need to hide anything when you come before Him. This woman had a devil at home and in her daughter. She was fed up to the teeth with the whole situation but I wonder how long she had actually been putting up with it until Jesus came along.

The girl was definitely not a baby. The woman's neighbors had probably poured so much scorn on her child's weird behavior she could not wait to see an end to it. She saw a chance for her daughter to be free at last and she grabbed it. Freedom is a chance only you can take; a decision only you can make when you choose to.

A Setback

The story, however, seems to take a strange and comic twist after that because — as yet — *Jesus simply ignored this woman!* In spite of her earnest plea for mercy, He would not budge. Neither did He say even one word to this pitiful woman. Do you wonder why? So did I, and I am sure the disciples did too.

Here was this poor mother, with a daughter suffering greatly and desperately needing His help; but it looked as though she would be getting absolutely nothing from Him. It was as if His mind were miles away and His disciples had to urge Him to either do something about the woman's devil or send her back home, at the very least, to save them all from being publicly embarrassed.

When we get to this juncture, there is one noteworthy point we need always to keep in mind, and it is this: *God does not snub anyone, although it might sometimes appear otherwise.* He heeds the cries of all who call on Him, but it might take more time for Him to respond in some situations.

There is no record of anyone calling on God for help and failing to get an answer from Him — even in the case of this Canaanite woman, as we will see in the latter part of the story. For some, it might just take more time before they gain an audience with God. If you keep calling on God in spite of His silence and despite the daunting world around — the world that tries to shut you up — one day Heaven itself will come to a standstill because of you.

Do you remember blind Bartimaeus? They told him, "Don't make that kind of noise around here! Don't act crazy! Shut up and stop bothering God. He is probably too good for a nuisance like you." They wanted him to behave himself in public, but he kept crying and shouting for mercy until Jesus stopped and called for him. Then, the same fellows who had rebuked him began to applaud him for his courage. They said to him, "Cheer up! On your feet! He's calling you." (*Mark 10: 46-52*)

God is always about to call someone soon. If it's going to be you, you may have to keep calling on Him for now.

This woman kept crying after Jesus until even His disciples got frustrated and had to speak to Him on her behalf. Her prayers did not cease until, someday, some people who did not know her from Adam joined her in her petition.

You need to be persistent when it comes to walking with God: "They that wait upon the LORD shall renew their strength" (*Isaiah 40:31, KJV*). If you really need God to renew your strength, you might have to start waiting on Him patiently and not walk off in haste. Persistence is powerful.

"Enoch walked with God; then he was no more, because God took him away." (*Genesis 5:24*) The man pressed so much into God's presence, God decided to have him stay for keeps. He wouldn't have to come as a visitor again.

If it looks as though God is ignoring you, the truth is that He is just waiting to see how far you will go in pursuing Him. Why? Because He wants your undivided attention more than you need His miracle. This is a fundamental truth. You, on your part, desperately want what He can give; but He, on His part, desperately wants *you*.

One day Enoch went on a trip with God and did not come back home again. When he was reported missing, everyone in his neighborhood suggested they call God's number. They said He was the only friend Enoch hung out with. So the search and rescue team took the advice and, true enough, when they called at God's place they found a note that read: *"Enoch walked with God and he was no more."*

Jesus kept walking away but this woman kept pursuing Him — and everyone in the street wondered why she would not just give up, give in, and go back home. You see, the world is free to wonder why you won't stop asking — and you are free to wonder why they won't start asking too. If they ask why you are so devoted to God, you should ask them how come they are not. You may want to let them know you are so sorry they are not informed about what you have found out: that God is the only true clue to all of life's puzzles.

Jesus is the only *genuine* way to God; that is why He is The Way, The Truth and The Life. There are many other claims and many other ways, but they all lead nowhere but to despair. Only Christ leads us back to God and to eternal life. He is the Password while all others are mere fibs. Many times you may have to persist until you can bring Him on board your life.

The world definitely cannot deny the power of God; and, if you will not give up, they will come on board on day, joining forces with you and your petition. Look around and you will see Peter, James, John and the other disciples beginning to speak up on behalf of this woman, where only a while ago they had merely watched and wondered.

Then the suspense began to mount, and Jesus had to say something — but not yet to the woman, and I wonder why. He just wouldn't speak to her. He turned to His disciples and said, "I was sent only to the lost sheep of Israel." And that was it! Passed over! This woman appeared to be no better than the scum of the earth, totally undeserving of any help from God. And the label on the delivery package read, "For the lost sheep of Israel only"; not "For everyone, such as a Canaanite woman in the vicinity". Whoa! Where then were those "lost sheep of Israel"? What had they been doing all that time, while this woman was trying to lay claim to the package that belonged to them?

Humility

God definitely has a special preference for His own, and He will move mountains just to bless them, no doubt about that. The problem, however, is that these special people of His are always nowhere to be found, especially at the most important moments. Although it is a small world, somehow, they just keep getting out of touch.

In Christ's quest to deliver the children's goodies, a smart dog crossed His path. She was so smart that, after some time, she noticed He had begun to discuss her with His disciples. There and then she drew nearer to hear Him and, while prying, she found out the reason for the long silence.

The power of God, primarily, was for the benefit of His children — those "lost sheep of Israel". "Oh! That's it," she must have exclaimed to herself — and immediately she devised a very clever follow-up strategy.

She drew close to the unrehearsed Jesus-and-His-disciples' conference and knelt down. She broke into the conference and paid homage. And, there in front of the Savior, lay prostrate another woman with a right and powerful attitude.

Nothing can stop people who, like this woman, know how to find their way through to God. However, to see God moved to action, one must be humble in heart and attitude.

> Though the LORD is on high, he looks upon the lowly, but the proud he knows from afar.
>
> *Psalm 138:6*

> The LORD detests all the proud of heart. Be sure of this: they will not go unpunished.
>
> *Proverbs 16:5*

The Lord keeps the proud at arm's length. This woman came and knelt down before Him; and, in so doing, she covered a great distance between herself and God. Humility is an effective strategy that anyone who needs Heaven's attention must add to her employ. Apart from God's mercy and your worship, something else is just as vital. It is called humility.

She was a smart woman! She did not just stand there aloof after breaking into God's presence. She knelt to pray the same prayers she had always prayed. She had been humiliated but she was not offended or discouraged. She remained humble and she was not too tired to pray again.

Note that she did not come to impress; the way she carried herself was not imposing. Her strategy paid off. God would not detest a humble person, so she was invited into the meeting as soon as she went on bended knees. There and then Jesus stopped talking to His disciples and turned to her. One-on-one, He gave her the attention she had always wanted. He said to her, "It is not right to take the children's bread and toss it to their dogs."

Not for Dogs!

Certainly, something was not quite right there all the while; otherwise, why would Jesus and His disciples even need to discuss who was to get the "children's bread" — the good things of God reserved for the Israelites? Yes, it is improper and unfair for fathers to hurl their children's food to their pets. It's not done! But would it be fair to deprive the dogs, in a situation where the children are nowhere to be found and the dogs are desperate for the food? The goodies would definitely have to go to the dogs then!

If the children are hungry, it's only proper for them to come home to dine, isn't it? It's definitely not the right thing to do, but desperate dogs will always eat the children's meal as long as those children remain far from home. If you are God's child, don't you think it's high time you went home to dine? Everyone, including the woman herself, admitted it wasn't fair to throw the children's food to the dogs — but with a rider to it.

> "Yes, Lord," she said, "but even the dogs eat the crumbs that fall from their masters' table."
>
> *Matthew 15:27*

If the children own the dog, they should definitely be the dog's masters. But are they actually the masters in real life? I have met a number of children who live like slaves — princes who live like paupers. Why? It is because they are ignorant of their rights and privileges. What we know and what we don't know determine how well we get along in life.

This woman had a better understanding of her rights as a dog than the children of Israel had of their kingdom privileges — to their detriment. She knew she had a right to the crumbs that fell from the children's table, when the children did not even show that they knew they had a right to the bread on the table. She knew her rights and she claimed them… and then some.

If necessity is the mother of invention — as the saying goes — then wisdom is the father and prayer the midwife. This woman needed a miracle; and, though she was just a dog in the house, she had the humility to pray and the wisdom to turn the household rules to her favor. If we do not have godly wisdom and prayerful hearts, we will not be able to live successful lives when necessity presses in on us.

The woman's acumen was amazing; the way it surpassed that of many Jews of her time was unparalleled. How did she know that Jesus was not just one of the sons of David but the "Lord, Son of David"? She had an understanding of who Jesus really was, and of her kingdom rights and privileges, in a kingdom where she was an outsider and where the actual citizens did not know their rights. She accepted that, fine, she was a dog; that was quite alright with her. She agreed that the children should get preferential treatment but pointed out at the same time that the dogs had their own privileges too. Anyone could have all they wanted for themselves as long as they did not deny her what was hers.

Jesus could do only a few miracles in Nazareth because "no prophet is accepted in his hometown" (*Luke 4:24*). Those folks in His hometown were among the privileged children mentioned above, and in fact had special claims to God's miraculous power. Mighty miracles could have taken place among them if only they too had acknowledged Jesus as Lord and reached out in faith. But they did not. So the "dog" — the Canaanite woman — ate their bread while laying claim to her crumbs.

Any "dog" that understands its place, rights and privileges will rule over children who lack kingdom understanding in such matters, notwithstanding their familiarity with the Father. What is the level of your kingdom intelligence? Are you sure the "dogs" on your street don't know more than you do? If you are wiser, why are they doing better than you? What you don't know will be to your detriment.

Wisdom

Wisdom is supreme; therefore get wisdom. Though it cost all you have, get understanding.

Proverbs 4:7

Buy the truth and do not sell it; get wisdom, discipline and understanding.

Proverbs 23:23

The Bible teaches us the wisdom that is from God. Read the Book of Proverbs; it will blow your mind with its wealth of information and ideas. Every time you find a new revelation from God's Word, you actually find a new lease of life. The world of the Word is a world where all things are possible with God. Obedience to what is written in the Word gives life.

Anyone who lives a prudent life will reign with champions. Champions rarely give excuses as to why they did not live up to expectations. Making excuses only gets you excused. Start investing in worthy information. Invest in a Study Bible; read it alongside other books written by great minds, especially believers. Daniel was a well-read man who gained much wisdom and understanding from books.

We need to learn from the right sources — that is, wherever the true Word of God serves as the benchmark for all that is being said and done. Many believers are deficient in faith because they have stagnated; they will not look to fresh sources of information or wisdom, or even learn anything new, preferring to remain stuck in their old mindsets all their lives.

Buy wisdom and don't sell it; ignorance costs you more than knowledge. Be wise!

164

Diligence

Lazy hands make a man poor, but diligent hands bring wealth.

Proverbs 10:4

Diligent hands will rule, but laziness ends in slave labor.

Proverbs 12:24

The sluggard craves and gets nothing, but the desires of the diligent are fully satisfied.

Proverbs 13:4

It takes diligence to gain wisdom; you need to put in time and effort to read your Bible and also good books from which you can acquire unique wisdom and knowledge. This is necessary for success in whatever endeavor you undertake. Most times you will not know what to do if you do not have the necessary information and understanding, and you will not know how to do it if you do not have the wisdom to go about it. Hence, if you are too lazy to acquire wisdom and do not make the effort to learn, you will always be poor and live a miserable life. So, what are we waiting for? Start learning, period!

You may feel like the underdog; you may feel that you belong to the underprivileged class and there is no way you can take the helm in the affairs of life. However, if you acquire wisdom and understanding, you will always get a good chance to be a winner too. There is always a point where you will break through to the other side, as the woman of faith did.

You cannot separate faith from godly wisdom and understanding; otherwise you will be beating against the wind. How can you believe what you don't know? Don't forget it is divine and not human wisdom or understanding that makes all the difference. Work hard to gain wisdom and understanding, for ignorance costs so much more than knowledge.

Bread is bread, in whatever form it comes — whether as a whole loaf or in crumbs. Really, the crumbs are the dog's privileges and the loaf belongs to the children but, every now and then, I get to see many dogs eating whole loaves and many children clamoring for the crumbs. I can only wonder when places and privileges were exchanged.

Immediately this woman made her case, Heaven applauded and the devil in her daughter had to leave — simply because a dog understood her rights in the world of children. This woman did not go home with crumbs that day but with a whole loaf.

If you look around today, you will find a great number of successful people who are not believers of the Christian faith but they are "believing" and achieving success in this temporal world — because they are the dogs who understand their rights and privileges, and thereby are getting the whole loaves.

All Achievers Are Believers

All achievers are "believers", in that they believe in someone or something. "Believers" are not necessarily Christians; some do have a strong faith in God but others place their trust in some other person or object. Some Christian preachers and writers even cite renowned infidels as examples of how to live an achiever's life. What a shame! We need to enlighten these people whom we now parade as "motivational speakers" in the church today.

There are more than enough role models in the Bible to draw upon, should we need examples of achievers. We have only to look to the great patriarchs and saints of God, such as Abraham, Joseph, Moses, Joshua, David, Solomon, Peter and Paul, James and John, to name but a few. There are also more than enough examples of achievers among the many faithful Christians living today, who are making a powerful impact on our contemporary world. You don't have to compromise to make a difference!

What could you possibly want to say that you cannot draw your examples from the life and principles of Jesus? He is the quintessence of all truths. We have lost our Christian heritage, and it is little wonder that the world makes fun of us; even up till today we have not made any difference that they can see.

To be truthful with you, however, you stand a better chance of making a meaningful impact on the world if you are a believer in God. Joseph made it in Egypt, far away from home. All he had was a large and faithful heart. Daniel and the other three Hebrew boys — Shadrach, Meshach and Abednego — were champions in the hostile kingdom of Babylon, far away from their home country. So was Esther; do you remember the orphan who became queen in place of Queen Vashti?

Yes, we do not belong here; we are in search of a heavenly city whose architect and builder is God. But we are not supposed to be merely mediocre while we are here on this earth. We can pull down intimidating walls of limitations and break down strongholds of the enemy. We can administer justice and seek the fulfillment of God's promises. We can shut the mouths of lions and quench the fury of the enemy's flames. We can generate strength in the place of weakness. We can win by wisdom and faith.

The principles of faith remain the same from age to age, and they are still as powerful and effective as ever. They will enable you to do great exploits for God while you are here. When we get to see God in Heaven, the just will not live by faith anymore; so now is your only chance to exercise your faith.

Although faith is only relevant here on earth, the children have a problem of being out of reach and the dogs always take advantage of this to get their privileges. Some children don't know their rights, neither do they live the life that produces tangible results and, in no time at all, smart dogs have eaten the good bread while foolish children go hungry.

Let us claim our heritage as children of God by understanding and employing kingdom principles in our daily living. Such principles include being diligent, consistent and faithful, understanding the place and power of God's mercy, persevering in prayer and supplication, and living a godly life.

The simple difference between unbelievers and believers in Christ is the salvation of the soul; that is the only thing we will attain that unbelievers will not, unless they get Born Again too. We have God's guarantee of eternal life but the package deal we get, when we accept Jesus as our Lord and Savior, also makes provision for living our lives here on earth.

The difference between the illustrious person and the nonentity is the knowledge each possesses and puts to use. The difference between the kingdom achiever and the non-kingdom achiever is faith — and the kingdom knowledge the former possesses and puts to use. Smart dogs may eat good bread but smart children will get to eat something even better. If you allow dogs to have first dibs at the buffet while you dawdle around, you may end up the big loser.

CHAPTER 7

What's on Your Mind?

What are you thinking of?

*What you have on your mind is more important
than what is happening around you.*

The Decision Is Yours

> A ruler came and knelt before him and said, "My daughter has
> just died. But come and put your hand on her, and she will
> live." Jesus got up and went with him, and so did his disciples.

Matthew 9: 18-19

In this account, a ruler named Jairus came calling on Jesus
for help. But before he said anything at all, he knelt down,
like the Canaanite woman in the previous chapter. He bowed
before Jesus the moment he gained entrance into His
presence. This ruler was not ashamed to worship a greater
Ruler in public, and probably right before the very eyes of
people over whom he exerted his own authority.

Before dealing with any other business, this man attended
to worship; thereafter he told the Lord his problem. The
situation he was in — his daughter had just died — did not
call for panic as long as he could gain access into God's
presence. He had his struggles but you would hardly know it,
so confident was he in God's ability to help him that he
appeared to be unperturbed by his crisis. Right inside him, he
must have figured out the solution; so, why trouble the world
with his struggles when he could get straight to the answer?

More important than the death of his daughter was his appointment with the Master of Life. More important than the crises life brings along our path is our appointment with the Master of the universe.

He told Jesus, "My daughter has just passed on *but* it doesn't matter much now. As long as you're around, it's not over yet."

No matter what happens to you, it's not over yet if God hasn't said it is. The world may crumble and your walls may fall apart, but it surely cannot be over if God hasn't declared it to be so! Instead of running around in panic, you should put your mind and your heart together in faith and start seeking the Master.

You are free to say, "Christ, my daughter just died *but…*"; "I just lost my job *but…*"; "I just got a bad report from my doctor *but…*" — or similar words, as long as you end with a "but" clause. It doesn't matter if something goes wrong as long as we can make sure it doesn't finish wrong at the end of it all. When you are discussing your troubles with God, never forget to put a "but" clause behind all you have to say; such as: "*But* come and put your hand on her, and she will live"; "*But* you can give me an even better job"; "*But* you can heal me".

Behave like one who knows nothing before the One who knows everything. And that is exactly what we are. We can't compare with God in knowledge, so we have no right to pronounce the final verdict on our life situations. What do you know? Little or nothing! Believe this and let God have the last say!

Be smart enough to give God a chance in every situation in your life, no matter how bad it gets. Give Him enough breathing space to work the miracle you need. Give every blow you get a "but": I am broke *but* I am getting rich as soon as I am done with being broke; I am sick *but* I am getting a clean bill of health as soon as I get through to God. The ruler knew that, where his daughter's life was concerned, it was Jesus — not Death — who would have the final say. She could still come alive though her body lay lifeless on her bed.

Do you know that, beyond death, there is life? Beyond failure, there is success. Beyond poverty, there is wealth and prosperity. Beyond your disappointments, there are other appointments. So do not stop. In this life, you have to keep moving ahead. You are almost there. Beyond that disease, there is a divine power that can heal you. Beyond every blow, there is a smile and, beyond every devil you come across in life, there is God. It all depends on where you choose to stop. And where you choose to stop depends so much on what's on your mind.

Failure is not the last bus stop along life's route. Winners keep moving on, and find that from there it's just a stone's throw to success.

Why do people quit before they reach their destination? Why do we linger around our failures at Losers' Alley? Why do we give up, when we can just pick ourselves up and keep moving till we arrive at Success Avenue? Now is never the time to stop and play dead. The odds you face in life will stop you in your tracks if you do not have a keen resolve to move on ahead. You must be willing to keep going on, knowing that peace awaits you after every storm and victory awaits you after every fight. Every champion has had to go one step further beyond failure. Every failure just didn't have the guts to take one more step forward. Life beckons beyond death. Success beckons beyond failure.

Listen to Jairus' words again: "My daughter has just died. *But* come and put your hands on her, and she will live." He definitely knew the solution to his problems before they came along; do you know yours too? When death did its worst, he did not think next about funeral arrangements but how to get his daughter a new lease of life. What is the first thing that comes to your mind when fiends from hell go on a rampage in your boulevard?

When some people fail, they start wondering if they will ever succeed again. And others, immediately they get sick, start thinking of dying and how they are going to fix their final will. You should rather think about triumphing in the face of failure and death, and surviving in the face of turmoil. This gives you an edge to pitch on the winning side. *Every winner has failed at least once and every loser has given up too soon.*

This man refused to call for his daughter's funeral until he had prayed for the restoration of her life. And, when he prayed, he did it decisively, not doubtfully. He not only asked Jesus to come and pray for his dead daughter, he actually asked Him to come and restore life back to her: "She is dead — fine! But I know that when you come onstage, the story will change; death will have to give way to life." Failure is not enough to discourage a winning spirit. Death cannot stop Life, *if you insist on winning and living.*

Now, if you set your mind on winning despite encountering defeats along the way, all Heaven will be on your side. God loves people who dare to win despite their failures. Jesus did not wait to ask who this fellow was; neither did He tell the man to wait while He wrapped up His meeting with John's disciples (He had been talking to them immediately before this incident). He agreed to come along at once. Why? It was because He found in this man a sure faith, and that excited Him greatly.

God is an optimist; He believes anything is possible. He is excited when He meets another optimist like this ruler — a man who had the optimism that is born of faith. Great stuff, this optimism; you need to get some of it for yourself!

You must keep holding on until you are declared a survivor. If you are not discovered with a mind already made-up, you may not be called to the champion's troupe. The moment a man of sure faith placed demands on Jesus, Heaven was set on a new course. Jesus got up and followed him, and the disciples followed suit. The crowd was left behind and anyone who cared to was free to come along. Why trouble yourself running around from pillar to post, when a living faith can bring God into your bedroom?

A More Powerful Resolution

> And, behold, a woman, which was diseased with an issue of blood twelve years, came behind him, and touched the hem of his garment.
>
> For she said within herself, If I may but touch his garment, I shall be whole.
>
> But Jesus turned him about, and when he saw her, he said, Daughter, be of good comfort; thy faith hath made thee whole. And the woman was made whole from that hour.
>
> *Matthew 9: 20-22, KJV*

Just then, as Jesus was on His way to restore the ruler's daughter to life, another General appeared on the scene — this time, a woman. In Chapter 1 of this book, we saw how Deborah showed up after Ehud. In the same way, here we see a woman showing up after the ruler Jairus — a woman with an even more powerful resolution than his.

She was a woman with an issue — *an issue of blood*. She had been bleeding for a long time, but her faith had not yet bled to death when Jesus came by. Deep within her, her faith was still alive and kicking. She did not have the courage to come openly, like the Canaanite woman we saw in the previous chapter (sometimes you too may not) but she had a simple resolution that would end her misery that day. She said, not to anybody — friend or foe — but to herself: "*If* I only touch the hem of His cloak, I will be well." *What do you say?*

That simple resolution was all she needed. It was enough to bring the King of kings to a halt. Till then, Christ had been on the move to get to the ruler's house, but He was not in too much of a hurry to slow down when a woman of faith crossed His path.

Whoa! Look how God is attracted to faith! He responds whenever and wherever He finds it — even a little grain of it — in people. There is enough power, even at the hem of God's garment, to work mighty miracles! Look at how this woman came through the back door to be blessed; all she needed was just a little faith, just a little touch, and it brought to an end twelve years of immense suffering! Whoa!!!

If she had told her friends what she intended to do, they would probably have laughed her to scorn. "You must be joking," they would have said. They would have advised her to get serious and behave reasonably, perhaps fix a special appointment with the Lord at another time when He was not too busy attending to others. But she did not listen to those naysayers. Instead, she listened to her own inner convictions; she had already resolved in her heart what she must do.

There is more to faith than what is seen on the outside. It derives its energy from within your convictions and not from any external appeal you may have. If you have faith you can interrupt God's business any day, any time. If you have faith you can determine the course through which the power flows. It is alright to confer with folks in a meeting but, when faith shows up, every deliberation comes to a close and God will then have the privilege of doing the extraordinary, which is His actual business.

All this woman had was a resolution in her heart, and she got her miracle before an energetic ruler did. She did not come to kneel before Jesus, as Jairus did; she did not even say a word of prayer. A resolution backed by action was all she had. Not stories of how badly she had suffered at the hands of her physician; someone else told those stories on her behalf. She came into church by the back door but with a mind fully resolved to get her miracle.

People without a strong internal resolve are the ones who spend the greater part of their physical energy and a large chunk of their time trying to find their way around life. When folks with powerful resolutions come onstage, they get straight to the point. It is your private resolve that determines how long you spend on the streets, struggling to overcome your problems and trying to make ends meet.

What do you believe deep down inside you? It has everything to do with what happens to you.

So What Are You Thinking?

We are meant to live *inside-out* and not *outside-in*. *Outside-in* means you are merely reacting to what is happening around you. You are not in control of situations but are just a victim of life, time and circumstances. You are being bullied and trampled on all around.

Inside-out, on the other hand, means you are compelling your environment to react to you and your own actions — those actions that are products of and motivated by the voices from within your soul and spirit-man. This way, you are the one who calls the shots; you are not a victim of life, time or your circumstances. It is the other way round; you are an actor and not a reactor. God's realm is resident within you, and you are allowing it to flow out of you to influence your environment.

This woman had been in pain for twelve years until a voice within her said, ***"This is your day!*** *You don't have to kneel down so He can lay hands on you. There is enough power in the hem of His garment.* ***Just go for it, as much as you want it!"*** Do you have a voice in your heart of hearts? What is it saying? What are you saying to yourself that no one but you and God can hear? What's on your mind?

Her thoughts triggered off a chain reaction; the moment the voice in her said, "Go for it", some virtue left Jesus and flowed into her body, even without His consent. Everything in Heaven gets activated on your behalf when your faith comes alive. *What's on your mind and what are the things you have been saying to yourself lately? Now is your time to go for it.*

Would not God have discovered it, since he knows the secrets of the heart?

Psalm 44:21

Above all else, guard your heart, for it is the wellspring of life.

Proverbs 4:23

As water reflects a face, so a man's heart reflects the man.

Proverbs 27:19

The good man brings good things out of the good stored up in his heart… out of the overflow of his heart his mouth speaks.

Luke 6:45

What are you thinking? Doctors might have discovered you have a terminal disease, but with God it is not time yet to start planning your funeral. Instead, you can start making plans to celebrate your miracle. Your pains can lead to gains; you do not have to come to a negative conclusion. Go positive on the negative because, with Jesus, you shall see positive results. Give God a reason to show up strong on your behalf.

There is enough power on the hem. You do not have to be the preacher's personal assistant; neither do you have to be well-known before God blesses you. You do not have to fast a million times to impress God — that little prayer in your room, that little devotion time, could be all you need if you come before Him with a sincere resolution in your heart.

If you believe God can pull you through, He will. You do not have to impress anyone in your cathedral with whatever. You do not even have to speak grammatically. It is not compulsory that you pray in the Queen's English. You can talk to God in your own dialect; He will hear you as long as you have resolved in faith to ask for His help. A faith-filled resolution is enough to bring Heaven on your side. What do you think and say to yourself when the chips are down?

But Jesus turned him about, and when he saw her, he said, Daughter, be of good comfort; **thy faith** hath made thee whole. And the woman was made whole from that hour.

Matthew 9:22, KJV

Notice that it was *her faith* and not even her touch that worked for her. Jesus said to her, "Daughter **your faith** (not your friend's faith and not your touch) has made you whole." It was her faith that motivated her to reach out and touch Him; it was her faith that sufficed in her encounter with Jesus. Anything can work if it is motivated by faith — whether it is a timid touch like this woman's or a bold request for home service like the ruler's.

As long as your faith is alive, nothing can be totally dead; or, even if it is dead — like Jairus' daughter — it can be revived. Your situation might not appear to improve right away, but it will be for just a moment. Before dawn, the darkness must disappear. Hopelessness must turn into gladness and everywhere it will be full of life again. Tell yourself, "It is just for a moment" and, as long as your mind is staying strong on God, by the time He is through with you, there will be more beautiful stories to tell than sad ones. Keep your faith alive and say these words to yourself:

> Finally, brothers, whatever is true, whatever is noble,
> whatever is right, whatever is pure, whatever is lovely,
> whatever is admirable — if anything is excellent or
> praiseworthy — think about such things.

Philippians 4:8

CHAPTER 8

The Next Level

A True Life Story

*Vagabondism becomes inevitable when folks decide
to set out on expeditions they were not divinely led
into and when they get involved in issues they
have little or no information about.*

The Unknown Levels

"They have taken my Lord away," she said, "and I don't know
where they have put him." At this, she turned around and saw
Jesus standing there, but she did not realize that it was Jesus.

"Woman," he said, "why are you crying? Who is it you are
looking for?"

John 20: 13-15

The very instant Mary expressed her desire to know her
Lord's whereabouts, Jesus emerged. When she affirmed how
desperate she was to find Him, He called her name. Anytime
when Heaven appears to be silent, it means something new
is about to transpire: something that has always been known
to God but is new to the person involved; something that is
going to take you to your next level.

Human life evolves in phases. Your next level is the next
phase of your life. It is always different from any prior
experience, and the best of it is only for anyone who is
willing to pay the price of waiting and reaching for it. These
next levels are designed to open doors to overwhelming and

total wellness as well as freshness for the persons involved, as long as they have learnt not to keep stumbling along in life. For every new phase of your life, God always has something entirely different from your old experiences. It will not only be new but, more importantly, it will infuse you with a greater verve.

Futile Ambitions

Now, as you coast along, it may amaze you to know that many times it is God's design to break you down in order to rid you of the inferior treasures you are still desperately holding onto. Though this may not be a delightful experience for you, it still needs to be done, when what you are attached to is nothing compared to what God wants to release to you.

What we obtain in eternity is more important than what we obtain in time.

All of us who set out on the expedition of life soon come to the crossroads where we must make choices for ourselves. At those crossroads, we have three options to choose from. The first is to live life as it comes. The second is to try to achieve our own ambitions, neglecting God's purposes for our lives. Funnily enough, many times we are judged to be "successful" when we pursue our own ambitions well enough. However, there is a third option: to choose to align ourselves with our Maker's purposes for us. This is the one option that absolutely consummates within us that sense of completion and fulfillment, without any regrets whatsoever, because it enables us to achieve what we were truly made for; and here is where we come to understand the true meaning of success.

Many times, however, it is only when we reach the level where we finally understand the futility of all human ambitions that we are ready to be directed into the process designed to make us true successes. All who understand the futility of their own ambitions and have aligned themselves with God's purposes would also have come to know that there is more to living than what we get and give.

Relationship is all; it is what determines our place in the present and in the future. More importantly, God is concerned about the relationship we maintain with Him, because this is what determines our place in eternity. As human beings, we are an eternal "going concern". Our time here on earth is simply a subset of our eternal life. And, out of everything we find while we are here on earth, there is only one thing we can lay hold of that we won't eventually lose at the end our life on earth. That one thing is either eternal life or eternal damnation.

Wills and Choices

Although some would not bother, most people would avail themselves of every opportunity life presents to them. Sometimes these opportunities do lead to great achievements, but why is it that many still cannot deny their own emptiness? This emptiness in us comes from doing what circumstances or people around us dictate that we do, as against doing what we know we were meant to do.

Life and mediocre folk are very good at bullying and ordering people around. Life naturally loves to make us live the way it dictates. It likes to rob us of the power to truly determine the outcome of situations in which we find ourselves. "That is life for you" — I hear people say that all the time. Unlike your regular waiter in a restaurant, who promptly gives you what you ask for, life does the opposite.

Before life grants you your heart's desire, it will always offer you what you do not want in the first place. And because many people lack the courage to say no and to follow their own personal convictions, they are left with no other choice but to live according to the precepts and dictates of powers beyond their control. Few have the true will to live as they deem fit and proper. More often than not, people are controlled by someone — such as a boss or a peer group — or something such as an addiction, or a physical or mental condition.

Truly all, who on their deathbed were glad about the way they had lived, would have at one time or another said "no" to this big bully called life. They would have refused to live their lives just the way it came. They would have made life come the way they desired it, by the power of their will and by making right choices. Yet, when all is said and done, a life lived like this still does not measure up to the best there is, if one has no hope of a new life in the hereafter — because there is yet a better option available.

Now, this is the better — in fact the best — option of all available to everyone: when we not only have the courage to say "no" to being bullied by life, but also the extra fortitude to hold our destiny up high in God's hand. All who have done this have been glad, when on their deathbed, about the life they had lived - *and also elated about the one they would be taking on in the hereafter.* And this is how God meant us to live our lives.

Some people are so much in love that they can't wait to get the object of their desire — and then, in their haste, they make wrong choices that are adorned in what seem to be the "right" colors. They are like Jacob (*Genesis 29: 16-30*): a man so much in love with Rachel that, while his friends went to medical school — in a manner of speaking — he slaved seven years for her father just so he could pay her dowry.

Yet, this same Jacob at the end of his servitude became so impatient to have Rachel that he didn't bother to confirm what was in the package he got before unwrapping it. That was how he ended up sleeping with Leah, Rachel's elder sister. What a trick! Laban is so much like life; though Jacob had worked himself out to pay his dues in life, Laban still defrauded him in a set-up. Nonetheless, it is important to note that it was not Laban who made him sleep with the wrong woman. Jacob made that choice himself, the night of his wedding.

He just wouldn't wait any longer. He was in so much of a hurry, he didn't check out the package first before going the whole hog. Alas, by the next morning, at the breaking of the dawn, behold it was Leah — but the deed had been done. He trusted the arrangement so much that he got what he didn't bargain for. It didn't come cheap at first, but now it felt good, it looked great, and it came easy — but it wasn't right because that wasn't what he had bargained for. Jacob had to live with the problems that came along with Leah for the rest of his life.

Patience is the strength that holds us down on the edge of the next level, till we are properly equipped to face up to life.

God also has beautiful packages for His people but He is never in a hurry to be pushed into unwrapping them. He ensures that you first learn all the truths you need for the time or experience in question. And, not being in any hurry to make His deliveries, He also tests and tries you before He discloses the details to you. Just jumping onto a feel-good bandwagon has led many astray, sometimes as far as forever.

The details of one's life are so crucial and fundamental that they cannot be explained to anyone who is not willing to wait, to listen and to learn. Otherwise, we can expect catastrophe as well. *Heaven would rather have a man set out uninformed than go wrongly informed.* If we are in a rush, we will miss important parts of the details. Such little mistakes have always resulted in generational damage since the days of the patriarch Abraham, who was resigned to having his servant become his heir; and when that did not work with God, he accepted a second offer of Hagar, his wife's maid.

God made sure the prophet Elijah fortified himself sufficiently for the strenuous task ahead of him. "Eat and drink now," He said to him, "for the journey is far." Those things that will last are not made in a hurry; those things that are unique are not mass produced.

Staying Strong

When it comes to staying strong on the tracks of life and purpose, it is not true to say that half a loaf is better than no bread. Rather, half a loaf is as bad as none at all. Only the whole loaf will do and nothing else. Champions are high fliers but there are no gas stations in the air; so, to avoid disaster, a high-flying captain should ensure that he has sufficient fuel for the whole stretch of his flight. God delights in taking you through life fully fueled for every time and purpose, every occasion, and every day. He helps us to do this by taking His time to prepare us on the edges of life.

These preparations take place in the dark nights: the periods between our dusks and daybreaks. What your life exhibits is a product of the type of encounters you had at the edges of every new experience you came into. You can soar greatly all the way despite the odds on your route, because you are well prepared, down to the smallest details. Or, you can come crashing down after taking off beautifully, because of what you have ignored. Others, however, stumble from beginning to end. Jumping the gun and ignoring the little details can lead to a woeful ending and irreversible losses. What is important is, after all, at your journey's end; you must not be worse off than you were at the start.

So how do we account for the vast difference we observe at the end of peoples' voyages? The answer lies in our attitude at the beginning of the journey. What we thought or did not think. What we did or did not do. Whether we were patient, or in a hurry and had no time to spare for God right from the beginning.

I wonder why anyone would choose to stumble along. Why would you just want to stumble in on God and stumble out, deciding to get the other details in the manual at your own later time? It is good that you take your time right from the beginning. Purpose is not a fifty-meter dash; it is a marathon. This part of this book is crucial because it explains something important about waiting on God before embarking on any major course of action in life. How much time do you have to spare, to invest in your future today? This is what determines how valuable you will be tomorrow. Time has its own advantages and the wise must learn to use it properly. There is no need to rush into a marathon!

> But they that wait upon the LORD shall renew their strength; they shall mount up with wings as eagles; they shall run, and not be weary; and they shall walk, and not faint.
>
> *Isaiah 40:31, KJV*

Every phase of life is a new beginning. There is a hierarchy in the spiritual realm and, for anyone who can keep in step with God, there is always a next level. God did not create us to settle down in one place, celebrating peanuts. He wants us to move on to higher and higher levels than ever before.

Rising Early... Due to a Nosy Heart

In the morning I lay my requests before you **and wait in expectation.**

Psalm 5:3

Early on the first day of the week, **while it was still dark,** Mary Magdalene went to the tomb and saw that the stone had been removed from the entrance. So she came running to Simon Peter and the other disciple, the one Jesus loved...

John 20: 1-2

In the morning – it is wise to deal with the practicalities of living as soon as possible. It is great to step out of an unreal world, which sometimes might even be our comfort zone, into the real world the earliest time we get the chance. It is good to look reality in the face before reality knocks on our door. All this can only be done if we take care to turn our focus in the right direction first. How do we do that? It is through seeking after the truth, verifying the facts, and understanding what is really important.

In *John 20: 1-2*, the most important objective was to revive a "dead and still dying" relationship – and it was the person coming earliest to the tomb who seized that opportunity. She saw the unusual: the *rolling away* of the mighty stone that stood between the Lord and the world for three days.

According to John's record, Mary Magdalene was the first person (apart from Heaven) to know that the stone sealing Jesus' tomb had been rolled away. Why? It was because she rose the earliest. She visited the tomb before anyone else did that day. She couldn't stay away; hungering after her Lord, she *had* to go nosing around His tomb. This hungry inquisitiveness is essential for anyone who wants to stay focused and keep in tune and in step with God.

How much are you willing to step out and try those things you think you know? Mary Magdalene had at one time in her life been subjected to the wicked influences of darkness before she met Jesus. She obviously had her own share of hell before she was delivered from the devils who had ruled over her.

You will acknowledge that it is horrible to have demons in your closet. Mary had them inside of her. Nevertheless, she was also the one who had the courage to walk alone to the "dead men's district" at an odd hour, all because she loved her new Lord. Her background knowledge of the existence of devils could not scare her anymore or keep her from fulfilling her strong desire to seek Jesus even among the dead.

A Question of Desire

Anything that would draw a woman out of her home at such an odd hour, to such an odd place, obviously had kept her from her sleep the night before. She must have had poor rest all night. There must have been a powerful prompting and probing in her mind, such a prompting and probing as would cause her to ignore the comforts of her bed. While every other person was snoozing away back home, she braved the thickest darkness in her quest for her Lord. Certainly, she had a heavy burden in her heart and a pressing question weighing on her mind.

Nothing can move us to do the unusual unless we are driven by an unusually strong desire. For Mary, what drove her was her desire to see Jesus again. For some, it may be a desire to succeed in a new area of their lives; yet others may simply want a revival. People who live complacent lives and desire nothing suffer from deficient minds. Such minds are not oriented towards progress; they are not purpose-driven. A life cannot be purpose-driven until it is fired by the desire to accomplish a worthwhile goal.

What is your goal? What is the burden in your heart and what is the desire that drives you? What is on your mind? Is anything weighing on your mind so much that it will cause you to rise early, just as Mary sought for Christ even at a time when He had lost His popularity among men?

Believe me; Mary went after an unpopular Savior — the Jesus who refused to prove His claims as King and who would not employ His powers to quell the public ridicule that eventually sent Him to the cross and to the crypt. But praise God it wasn't forever! It was but for a season and to accomplish a purpose! God had a goal. He also had strategies.

It takes a unique person to be a fan of such an unpopular champion, and the Captains of Life are often such unique people: they would rather follow their heart than go with the common flow. Do you have a burning desire in your heart that would make you do the most shocking thing anyone can ever think of? Like Hannah, a woman who prayed so earnestly her pastor thought she was drunk? (1 Samuel 1:9-16) Is there anything that burns so passionately in your spirit that it would deny you the comfort of your bed and the pleasure of your sleep? I must inform you that, until we come to the point where we cannot help but be ridiculous, we may not be ready for the miraculous.

Have you ever got so troubled you couldn't sleep, because you had not fellowshipped with God for the day? Yeah, it is possible to be close friends with God; He wants to talk with you all the time. Mary was worried about something: her Lord!

It had been three days since He was hushed by humanity. This same Lord was her Deliverer and He claimed to be her Savior. He was supposed to be Immanuel (God with her) but now He had been crucified.

Jesus had spoken about His death long before it happened; and indeed He did die. But there was something else He had talked about too — His resurrection on the third day. Perhaps Mary remembered that. It was now the third day and, quickly, she must go to His tomb! Peradventure He would do as He had promised. She had seen Him the day He was buried; then, the following day had been the Sabbath and she had been expected to remain indoors resting, away from all forms of work.

However, she must have kept pondering on Jesus' promise that He would rise on the third day. She was so eager to see the Lord that she could not wait till dawn before rushing to the place where she had last seen Him —

Anyone who remembers the Word of God is a potential champion.

the tomb. Where and when was your last encounter with God? Do you care to keep the relationship going?

Do you believe God meant business when He spoke a word into your life recently? There must have been something you heard God say to you recently, maybe in church, or through a friend or a preacher on television. I must tell you that God actually have you on His mind. You could be the next person on His agenda, but you will never be able to tell a fine story if all you do is sit down at home and watch the world go by. Declaring a grand and total war against a lifestyle of complacency and mediocrity is the first step towards productive living.

You really need to take a bold step towards God, disregarding the odds that threaten to obliterate His promises to you. You need to seek Him out. You must pray and connect with Him. Mary was curious about what was happening to her Lord after two days of silence. Although everybody shared the burden, she undertook a greater part of it. Others slept and waited, but she did not.

> A little sleep, a little slumber, a little folding of the hands to rest — **and poverty will come on you like a bandit and scarcity like an armed man.**
>
> *Proverbs 6:10*

> One who is slack in his work is brother to one who destroys.
>
> *Proverbs 18:9*

Now your restlessness, to a certain extent, is an indicator of the importance you attach to the goal you are pursuing. Conversely, how much you slumber also reveals the degree of importance — or unimportance — you attach to your business. The zeal with which we pursue our objectives attests to the significance of the goals we have set. If you esteem highly your appointments and purposes, you won't enjoy being complacent.

Always in Charge

> [A]nd saw that the stone had been removed...
>
> *John 20:1*

If she had not come to the tomb, she would not have seen and known about the removal of the stone. If you don't make your move, nothing moves for you. If you refuse to approach the practicalities of life, you will only know your impossibilities and not your possibilities. But, if you dare to step out, your chances as well as the odds will become clearer. However, in due season, insurmountable obstacles must disappear and cordons must be removed. Life's doors do not always stay shut. There is a time for them to be shut and a time for them to be opened wide; but you will not know this if, in the first place, you have not focused in their direction.

Jesus was not destined to remain quiet and dead in the tomb forever. God can't go into extinction. His set time was just for three days. He is the Truth and circumstances can't hold the Truth captive for too long. *Even in the grave, Jesus was Lord.* And, in sickness, He is the Healer. In pain, He is the Comforter. In distress, He is the Helper. In poverty, He is the One who prospers us; and, in failure, He is the Way to Success. A deteriorating life is not beyond His power to rejuvenate, and human failings only reveal God's power in greater measure. The daunting situations of life do not intimidate the true God. Satan is permitted to show off his crazy skills but his antics do not disturb God's agenda because, at the right time, God will show up to accomplish His purposes according to what He has said in His Word.

Hence, if we are complacent in spiritual matters, we will never know the mind of God. We will never know God's next agenda or the next stone He has moved, if we do not deliberately seek after Him. But if we seek Him, we will find Him — if we seek Him with all our heart. The spiritual and the physical have a melting point: that is the place where the issues of life pertaining to destiny and purpose are resolved. The roads that lead to success are fashioned for purpose-driven lives alone.

If you do not commit yourself in devotion towards God, you will never know the moving of the Spirit in your favor. It took a woman who would rise early to seek God against the odds, to know that the unusual had happened. She was that devoted; hence she was the first herald of the life-changing revelation of Jesus' resurrection — all because she came earliest.

It seems as though the idea of a quiet time with God is fast being battered by the demands of a commercial, internet and digital world, where everybody hurries and hustles to make ends meet and there is virtually no time left for reflection. But the people who still cherish the time they spend with God are the only ones who will have the privilege of enjoying a firsthand experience of God's activities at the next levels. Everything we know as it is today will melt away, just as the things we know from the past have melted away. The only sure thing is God's Word.

> Then the LORD replied: "Write down the revelation and make it plain on tablets **so that a herald may run with it.**
>
> *Habakkuk 2:2*

Until we discover the mind of Heaven, we will not live our lives at the right pace. The world is full of people going on a stroll and, while some others are on a run, it is only the ones with divine vision who have God's speed. When we are on course because we are in tune with the mind of God, we live life at a pace different from that of the world. This is because we are already seeing a divine vision different from what the world sees, and it is this vision that makes the difference. It is the revelation of the mind of God and it only comes to people who are willing to take a bold step into God's presence.

> I will stand at my watch and station myself on the ramparts; I will look to see what he will say to me, and what answer I am to give to this complaint.
>
> *Habakkuk 2:1*

So She Came Running

What gets us up and running? It is vision! It is the revelation of the unusual and the hearing of the uncommon. When you see a man on the move, watch it: it is either he has made contact with the unusual or he is competing in a game where failure or success comes at a price. *Vision is a driving force and it can make crippled legs spin faster than automatic wheels.*

Let us begin to focus rightly. Let us be committed to living a life motivated by divine insights today and tomorrow. If you endeavor to live a visionary life, you will not be preoccupied with irrelevance. The life of a man of purpose is rightly defined and is not cluttered with irrelevance and non-essentials.

Tears of Ignorance

"They have taken the Lord out of the tomb, and we don't know where they have put him!"

John 20:2

She had despaired because, upon getting to the place where she had last seen Jesus, she found the unusual had happened. The tide had turned. There had been a move of God. Now, it was true that she had sought God early and revered Him — but Jesus was no more in the tomb. Her timing was great but her focus was not to the point. The tomb is the last place to seek a Living Savior.

We may be setting our focus on the wrong places when we fail to fully appreciate the words of God. Many are still holding on to what they are familiar with from their past because they have not aligned themselves with the mind of God. If Mary had really believed that Christ was going to rise again on the third day, as He had said, I am sure she would not have been upset with the empty tomb; it would only have excited her.

Some of us may be fervent God seekers but our problem is that we get upset by the "empty tomb" situations we encounter in life. We panic when the unexpected happens, when we should be rejoicing because we are on the verge of a new level. Sometimes the same desire that drives us after God keeps us from appreciating the new level He intends to bring us to. We run out of steam when it looks like our earnest desires have only driven us to a dead end.

Why get upset when what we believe in becomes unpopular? All Mary could comprehend was "They have taken away the Lord." But, then, God is bigger than every human manipulation. He is the Rock of Ages and no human scheme is capable of moving Him away, as Mary had supposed. If you are in love with Him, your heart is in good hands because He will always be right where you need Him: immovable and unshakable.

But how miserable we will always be, when we do not understand from God's perspective!

She reported a sudden relocation of Christ out of the usual environment, but she lacked an understanding of the program that funded the movement (if there was any in the first premise). There wasn't a movement but a transformation; yes, and it was by no means a human funded operation — not *"they"*. It was a divine arrangement. The time will come, and indeed it is already here, when God will overrule all human set-ups. And you may even be in that season of your life now. Now is the time when God wants to show up strong on your behalf. Get ready. "The powers that be" may have driven you to a dead end, but your faith in God will not allow Him to forget you ever. When your back is against the wall, He will surely come and see you!

The promise of resurrection, the second phase of the redemption agenda, had just been fulfilled. Heaven is rejoicing, hell is in panic, and the whole earth is thrown into confusion. There is pandemonium and Satan can be heard screaming at his demonic generals, demanding: "How could you let that Man go! You have ruined us! You have allowed Jesus to be resurrected. I thought we had Him bound all this while! But see! He has broken through our ranks! See! He is resurrected!"

Today, to you who are reading this book, whoever you are, I would like to announce that the ranks of hell have been broken on your behalf. The power of God vindicates you, even now. Amen. Christ has overcome death! Glory to God!

It is interesting how some people insist on mourning when the situation actually calls for joy. The disciples called the Lord a "ghost" because He walked to their rescue on troubled waters. Isn't that funny? Sometimes our first reaction is fear when the Lord is actually helping us to triumph over our problems. Storms do come into our life but they are there only to showcase the majesty of God.

You should not give way to fear just because a situation appears scary. Some things are really not as harmful as they make themselves out to be. Jesus had been lifted from the ranks of dead men to life everlasting, but Mary cried because she thought it was all over for Him and inevitably for her. Those were tears of ignorance. Remember what was said of Him in the Old Testament, before He even came down to earth:

Because you will not abandon me to the grave, nor will you let your Holy One see decay.

Psalm 16:10

It was impossible for death to have any hold over the Lord of Life:

> But God raised him from the dead, freeing him from the agony of death, **because it was impossible for death to keep its hold on him.**
>
> *Acts 2:24*

Keeping in Step with God

> "They have taken my Lord away," she said, "and I don't know where they have put him."
>
> *John 20:13*

Sometimes, God has already gone far ahead from where we think He is. He has moved on, but we were unaware of it. This is one reason why we often get caught unknowingly in idolatry — because we have not been walking closely with the Lord and have not come to realize He has moved somewhere else ahead of what we know.

The same bronze snake that the Lord told Moses to make in the wilderness, for the healing of the Israelites, became an article of idol worship that needed to be destroyed by King Hezekiah. It was called *Nehushtan*, "an unclean thing".

> The LORD said to Moses, "Make a snake and put it up on a pole; anyone who is bitten can look at it and live." So Moses made a bronze snake and put it up on a pole. Then when anyone was bitten by a snake and looked at the bronze snake, he lived.
>
> *Numbers 21: 8-9*

> [Hezekiah] broke into pieces the bronze snake Moses had made, for up to that time the Israelites had been burning incense to it. (It was called *Nehushtan*.)
>
> *2 Kings 18:4*

God was no longer in the business of healing the Israelites through the bronze statue of a snake, but they still indulged the idea. Jesus had destroyed death but Mary did not know it.

There are no vacuums in the spirit and, if God is not occupying a place, Satan is. There is no grey area or middle ground in the spirit; it is either black or white. Many are clueless about what God is up to in their lives because they are too conscious of yesterday. Don't relax in places where God used to be with you. Don't go building monuments of idolatry in the name of religion, without bothering to find out if your actions are still in tune with God.

God transcends time; He is not subject to it. He resides throughout and in eternity. He said to Moses, when Israel was on the verge of a new level:

> And I appeared unto Abraham, unto Isaac, and unto Jacob, by the name of God Almighty, **but by my name JEHOVAH was I not known to them.**
>
> *Exodus 6:3, KJV*

The three people mentioned in this Bible passage were the patriarchs we all hold in high esteem today; but here God was revealing Himself to Moses in a way He had not revealed Himself to them. This does not imply that the patriarchs were totally ignorant of the name *Jehovah*; rather, the scripture indicates that they did not understand the full significance of the name that denoted the One who would redeem His people from bondage. The patriarchs did not live in the days of the taskmasters of Egypt, so they would not appreciate what it meant to have God as their great Deliverer.

God has a divine program designed for every season and every occasion. The kingdom pattern that applied to some circumstances in times past might not be relevant now. On the first occasion when God provided water in the wilderness for the Israelites, He told Moses to strike the rock with his staff:

> The LORD answered Moses, "Walk on ahead of the people. Take with you some of the elders of Israel and take in your hand the staff with which you struck the Nile, and go. I will stand there before you by the rock at Horeb. Strike the rock, and water will come out of it for the people to drink." So Moses did this in the sight of the elders of Israel.
>
> *Exodus 17: 5-6*

The second time round, however, God told Moses to speak to the rock. But the man of God again struck the rock and, though water still came forth for the people, God was not pleased. It cost Moses his future.

> The LORD said to Moses, "Take the staff, and you and your brother Aaron gather the assembly together. Speak to that rock before their eyes and it will pour out its water. You will bring water out of the rock for the community so they and their livestock can drink."
>
> So Moses took the staff from the LORD's presence, just as he commanded him. He and Aaron gathered the assembly together in front of the rock...
>
> Then Moses raised his arm and struck the rock twice with his staff. Water gushed out, and the community and their livestock drank. But the LORD said to Moses and Aaron, "Because you did not trust in me enough to honor me as holy in the sight of the Israelites, you will not bring this community into the land I give them."
>
> *Numbers 20: 7-12*

One thing consistent about God is that He is not restricted in the way He operates. He is dynamic. To be compliant in spiritual matters, you must stay constantly in tune with His Holy Spirit in prayer and in your devotions.

We have to come early into His presence: alone, to a quiet place to inquire of Him. You may be the next person to receive a revelation or idea from God that will turn the world upside down. You may be the next person God wants to use to turn the world "right-side up".

The Jump Starter and the Latecomers

> Early on the first day of the week, while it was still dark, Mary Magdalene went to the tomb and saw that the stone had been removed from the entrance. So she came running to Simon Peter and the other disciple... and said, "They have taken the Lord out of the tomb, and we don't know where they have put him!"
>
> So Peter and the other disciple started for the tomb. Both were running, but the other disciple outran Peter and reached the tomb first.
>
> *John 20: 1-4*

Peter and John would not have begun their race to the tomb, but for the persuasion of a woman. They might not have been sleeping when Mary set forth for the Lord's tomb; still, they did not have the testimony of being the first on the scene.

They were supposed to be the leaders in charge. They should have been the ones to lead the crew; but they failed. Leaders set the pace at which others advance, but they failed to do so. Instead of initiating the race, they were latecomers. A woman chose to seek the Lord earlier than they did; she rose earlier and became the jump starter, triggering the others to start their race. Through her testimony, she motivated the other disciples, including Peter and John.

Both were running, but the other disciple outran Peter and reached the tomb first. But now it no longer mattered who came first. Among latecomers, all are equals: they are all late. None will ever have the distinction of being the first on the scene. That honor belongs to the jump starter.

Diligence and Pace Setting

Many times, if we refuse to act quickly, someone else —
often the most unlikely person — might take our place as the
jump starter. How long will you keep God waiting for you?

> Finally the other disciple, who had reached the tomb first, also
> went inside. **He saw and believed.** (They still did not
> understand from Scripture that Jesus had to rise from the
> dead.)
>
> *John 20: 8-9*

In his Gospel, the Apostle John gave an impartial account of
our Lord's resurrection. John did not gloss over his failings
but owned up unashamedly to the state of his faith at the
time, as that of one who had to "see to believe". He had yet
to learn, as he did later, that "the just shall live by faith and
not by sight or hearing".

The Apostle John had to see to believe because, in those
days, he did not know the invincible Word of God that says
Jesus must rise from the dead. This could explain why he did
not bother to visit the tomb up till then. He did not believe in
the resurrection and must have felt everything was over with
the crucifixion.

There is an obvious difference between a believer and an
unbeliever. The former is a pioneer and an achiever, a major
player on the winning team, whilst the latter is merely a
spectator who pays to watch the game.

Believers are adventurous by nature and they love to go
off the beaten path, whilst unbelievers are skeptics who will
only go on safe tours. Many unbelievers do not understand
the Bible; they build tall, thick walls around their own small
world, and they would rather continue living in mediocrity
and obscurity than take a chance with God.

God Is Not Garrulous

Someone once said you have to *hear and hear...* before you can believe. What a great truth! But what does it mean? Has God become a chatterbox or stutterer that He has to keep repeating Himself before He can make sense? No! *God is not talkative but you must hear His word continuously.* That is how faith is built. And that is how you stay in tune with Him.

> Consequently, faith comes from hearing the message, and the message is heard through the word of Christ.
>
> *Romans 10:17*

Many find it hard to believe in God because much of what they hear from the preacher's pulpit is mere human philosophy, psychology or sentiment. If what you are hearing is really the Word of God, it will definitely produce faith in you. To have faith, all you need is God's Word and a good heart. Nobody ever heard God's voice and remained the same, except those who are given over to the enemy because of the wickedness in their hearts.

Moses said, "We have met with the LORD **and He says...**" (*Exodus 5:3*). God's Word is the reason a fugitive like Moses could become a national leader. When a man encounters God, he receives the authority to make demands on "the powers that be":

> God hath spoken once; twice have I heard this; that power belongeth unto God.
>
> *Psalms 62:11, KJV*

There is a difference between those who take the Word of God into their hearts and those others who have just head knowledge of what is documented in the Bible. John, for example, was caught off guard because of what he did not yet know in his heart. The doings of God will always puzzle those who do not know Him and do not pay attention to His Word.

If you are not attuned to God's mind as revealed in the Bible, you will be surprised if not disappointed when He moves on to the next level. Where was John all the while when Jesus was talking about His resurrection? Was he paying attention at all? What is the benefit of your going to church? Is it the fine lady or the great guy you met there? The fine shoes and clothes a friend just got or the worship, fellowship and Word of God?

Jesus said, "Blessed are those who have not seen and yet have believed." (*John 20:29*) There is a blessing that comes with believing God in spite of circumstances that appear to contradict His words.

> Blessed is she who **has** believed that what the Lord has said to her will be accomplished!"
>
> *Luke 1:45*

She was blessed because she had believed the Lord's words, no matter how impossible they seemed! *Achievers are believers and believers are achievers.* Nothing is as exciting as seeing the impossible happen, when it is the result of what you have believed and desired in faith, and it is in line with God's purposes for you. Such a great blessing is the work of faith.

Nothing is too farfetched that faith cannot make tangible. It might not happen instantly but, before you know it, what you believe has already become real. Believe God for something today, and you will realize that a faithless life is a substandard one. You are functioning below your capacity when you operate without faith. The reason you are no better than what you are now is that you have never thought of becoming better; or, if you did, you couldn't fathom it in faith.

Today is always the future we believed in yesterday and, as long as there is a tomorrow, the future will not hesitate to come to us. However, the future that arrives at our doorstep tomorrow is what we invest in today. What you have in your mind's eye today will be birthed forth in the future you call tomorrow. So, let us begin now to work for and towards life ahead. Let us do it in faith and have some fun while we are here on this earth, living within the confines of time.

The Correct Combination

You will discover God's will for your life when you devote yourself to reading and studying His Word. You can live a life that works by believing the promises you will find in the Bible; they are real! Nothing is impossible! God is the God of all righteous possibilities. If you can think of it, you can believe it. If you can believe it, you can achieve it. Anything that crosses the mind of man is possible. As long as it is done in true faith, you *will* get it.

> "I tell you the truth, if anyone says to this mountain, 'Go, throw yourself into the sea,' **and does not doubt in his heart but believes that what he says will happen,** it will be done for him. Therefore I tell you, **whatever you ask for in prayer,** believe that you have received it, and it will be yours."
>
> *Mark 11: 23-24*

Believers are able to achieve the impossible because their faith generates abilities that produce results. Such results are otherwise not humanly attainable; the only reason for their achievement is that the achiever is a believer. So, literally, a believer is dynamic and unlimited by the physical realm.

It is a great blessing when you are not limited to what your mind can grasp alone. The day you start living beyond your imagination is the day you started believing. Man may know your past but they will never be able to tell your future when you become a believer.

Characteristics of Believers

Believers remain unperturbed by what is happening around them because there are greater things happening inside them, that are about to erupt out of them and change their world. You may not look special on the outside but, inside, you are full of wondrous possibilities.

You are created to be amazing and, if you believe you are, you must henceforth begin to live the life of a believer. Don't look on the outside, look on the inside. Don't trouble yourself with the cable news and the newspaper reports. Believe God's Word and look into the perfect law of liberty as you observe His Word daily. Don't go walking from one place to another, looking for what you can see before you can believe; rather, start thinking about what you can believe to see happen.

People who wait to see before believing do not have claims to the miraculous. By the time they start seeing, they will not see the fantastic; they will only see the commonplace. The extraordinary, on the other hand, is seen only by people in whom faith functions before sight.

Characteristics of Latecomers

Latecomers tend to experience only the snippets, because their sight functions before their faith. Latecomers arrive in a hurry and then they excuse themselves in no time. They are people who come to see what another person has dared to discover while it was yet unpopular.

Latecomers usually turn up in a bid to substantiate another person's claim. They never have a story of their own. They echo others' voices by speaking and behaving in like manner. They are impostors. Their activities are founded on the pedestals of another person's passion. They don't have first-hand information but only the leftovers from others. As a result, they are prone to becoming extinct in no time at all.

A durable structure can never be constructed on another person's edifice; it has to be constructed on its own foundation. For your assertions to stand the test of time, they must have a proper, unique and sure foundation. The serious-minded will never allow the success of their venture to be predicated upon the decisions others make for them. If you build your destiny on another's edifice, you can be sure the end of that edifice also marks the end of your destiny. Build only on the one sure foundation, which is Christ. Build in faith and with a vision.

Many fall away from their faith because they have role models other than Christ and, when their role model falters, they falter too and they get discouraged. I have noticed that people who behave like their role models often struggle with appreciating who they really are. Why must you act like someone else? Why should you be a replica of another?

All of us are different and unique, but not all of us appreciate our own uniqueness. It is common to see people copying the mannerisms and way of life of their role models; they would rather be a copy of someone else than the original that God made them to be. These people lack the courage to discover themselves and what their purpose in life really is.

Yes, we have much to learn from other people, especially those who have succeeded in endeavors similar to what we desire to accomplish. However, we shouldn't try to be like them. All of us have our own unique identity in God and, if you want to be like someone else, I have only this to say to you: "You've got to be joking; the best you can be is a runoff and, when the original ceases to be relevant, you also will cease to be." Now you see what I mean: having a mentor is not about giving up your own identity!

But One Father

"And do not call anyone on earth 'father', for you have one Father, and he is in heaven. Nor are you to be called 'teacher', for you have one Teacher, the Christ. The greatest among you will be your servant."

Matthew 23: 9-11

We have but one Father. He is the only true God and Father of our Lord Jesus Christ. He is Jehovah. We may have many guardians of our faith, but only one Father — and that is God. Those guardians teach us what we don't know and guide us through paths they have walked before us, but we should not behave or become like them. Otherwise, we will have many people who are no more than duplicates of others.

Meanwhile a Jew named Apollos… came to Ephesus. He was a learned man, with a thorough knowledge of the Scriptures. **He had been instructed in the way of the Lord ... and taught about Jesus accurately, though he knew only the baptism of John...**

When Priscilla and Aquila heard him, **they** invited him to their home and **explained to him the way of God more adequately**. When Apollos wanted to go to Achaia, the brothers encouraged him and wrote to the disciples there to welcome him.

Acts 18: 24-27

We are not and must not claim to be an authority whatsoever in matters of faith. Nevertheless, we must be willing to share what we do know with others. We must always be willing to instruct them and listen to what they have to say and, if necessary, encourage them. We must also be ready to learn from reputable people — just like Apollos, who though a learned man was eager to learn from Priscilla and Aquila.

They Went Back as Soon as They Came

> He [Simon Peter] saw the strips of linen lying there, as well as the burial cloth that had been around Jesus' head. The cloth was folded up by itself, separate from the linen...
>
> Then the disciples went back to their homes, but Mary stood outside the tomb crying.
>
> *John 20: 6-7, 10-11*

Despite momentous events taking place right before their eyes — the empty tomb, the burial cloths folded up by themselves, the absence of Jesus' body — the disciples did not bother to investigate these strange phenomena. They simply went back home just the way they came!

That's it! Latecomers are never fully persuaded by the extraordinary. They rarely care that much. They will not stay to see history take place — those significant moments when old records are broken and new ones set. They would have gone back home!

Yes, the disciples were moved, but not to the point of wanting to discover what had happened to Jesus and why He was no longer in the tomb. I wonder what John was thinking when he saw the empty tomb. Did he really believe Jesus had been raised from the dead? Why then did he not wait to find out His whereabouts? Or, did he go to the tomb merely to confirm Mary's news about the Lord's sudden disappearance and, once he had done that, he felt his duty was done and it was time for him to go back home?

How about Peter? Despite the race to get to the tomb and his haste to enter first, his zeal soon petered out... and he went tamely back home. Disregarding the strange sight of the empty tomb and unwilling to investigate further into the matter, he returned to the place from which he had started running. Latecomers are not people who deliberately set out after God. They won't last long on the scene and there may be nothing anybody can do about that.

The Cutting Edge

There is always a turning point, the place where God unveils new, mind-blowing revelations and cutting-edge experiences. Many people don't have the guts to hang around such places because of the radical nature of these experiences. Latecomers always come to see but not to conquer. You should never be deceived by their presence because, in next to no time, they will go back home like the majority in Gideon's army.

> The LORD said… "Anyone who trembles with fear may turn back and leave Mount Gilead." So, twenty-two thousand men left, while ten thousand remained.
>
> But the LORD said to Gideon… "Take them down to the water, and I will sift them for you there… Separate those who lap the water with their tongues like a dog from those who kneel down to drink." Three hundred men lapped with their hands to their mouths. All the rest got down on their knees to drink.
>
> The LORD said to Gideon, "With the three hundred men that lapped I will save you and give the Midianites into your hands. Let all the other men go, each to his own place."
>
> *Judges 7: 2-7*

God knew it was better to excuse the latecomers in Gideon's army before they reached the battlefront; otherwise they would have bred disaster with their inevitable and sudden desire to be excused from the ranks, especially in the heat of the fighting.

How many times have we backed out when on the edge of a conquest? This is a question we must, each of us, ask of ourselves and answer truthfully, if we want to know how well we are faring in our quest for purpose and the fulfillment of our destiny.

Yes, it does get darker at the edge of a new dawn; but it is a mistake to walk away at the very point when your breakthrough is about to happen.

We need to hold on to our faith; losing it is unthinkable. We must also learn how to keep moving on, for stagnation is acutely detrimental to the fulfillment of great destinies. We cannot afford to stay out of God's reach for one moment. We must therefore guard against the faithlessness and lack of commitment that keep us out of God's reach.

We must not lose faith, because without faith it is impossible to please God. Stay in God's presence, you are almost there. Why are you in a hurry to go elsewhere? The tomb — the place where we seem to have buried our hopes and dreams — is actually the turning point, where God intervenes and initiates cutting-edge experiences that will take us to a whole new level. God never hesitates to reveal Himself in a new way to anyone who cares to wait on Him, especially in trying circumstances where we are actually on the edge of great groundbreaking changes.

The principles of God are consistent but their applications are dynamic.

On the edge there is always a period of silence: a period of time that demarcates what used to be from what is to begin, the old from the new, the usual from the unusual; that distinguishes between the ways of God amongst us in times past and the time when prophecies and promises are on the verge of fulfillment.

Many have missed fulfilling their God-given purpose and many more will miss it because they lack the courage to wait for it. They lack the guts to say no to distraction.

Old Simeon

Now there was a man in Jerusalem called Simeon, who was righteous and **devout. He was waiting for** the consolation of Israel, and the Holy Spirit was upon him. It had been revealed to him by the Holy Spirit that he would not die before he had seen the Lord's Christ. Moved by the Spirit, he went into the temple courts.

When the parents brought in the child Jesus to do for him what the custom of the Law required, Simeon took him in his arms and praised God, saying:

"Sovereign Lord, as you have promised, you now dismiss your servant in peace. For my eyes have seen your salvation, which **you have prepared in the sight of all people,** a light for revelation to the Gentiles and for glory to your people Israel."

Luke 2: 25-32

Simeon's desire to see the Messiah was strong enough to avail to him the privilege of living until he had seen baby Jesus. He not only desired to see the prophecy fulfilled regarding the coming of the Christ; he also watched and waited for it.

"For my eyes have seen your salvation, which you have prepared in the sight of all people." Now, the eyes of anyone who waits for **it** will not be denied the privilege of seeing **it.** It intrigued me when I discovered that this salvation Simeon saw was not classified information. It was prepared in the open, in the sight of all. The Christ project was not restricted to just a privileged few; Jesus came for the benefit of all mankind. What then amazes me even more is the fact that only a few people caught the revelation.

The dealings of God are not secretive. Heaven has nothing to hide. Nonetheless, it does not mean everyone will be interested or able to understand what God is doing.

The Bible is the Word of God and it reveals the mind of God. It is also the most popular book in the world today and the most enduring through all ages; but such popularity does not necessarily mean that the mind of God is as popular as the Book is. This is because only a few care to delve deep into it and act upon the reality of its contents. All who diligently desire new revelations from God will receive them, if they would only stand and act upon His Word.

Hanging Around

Now, others may leave but Mary would not. She could not afford to move without precise information about Jesus' whereabouts. Where would she go anyway, when the only place she ever wanted to be was where her Lord and her love led her? She did not know where Jesus was, so she waited outside the place she had last seen Him.

Not a word from her until she heard her Master's voice again. Mary did not make one more move thereafter, until she found the Teacher's footprints. She would not lift her hands or vent her emotions until she broke into her next level, the place where the Spirit was present and operating.

Vagabondism becomes inevitable when folks decide to set out on expeditions they were not divinely led into and when they get involved in issues they have little or no information about. But Mary would rather wait in the place of her last encounter with her Lord than move around aimlessly, without divine direction and informed leadership. She waited until God came and moved her into His next level for her.

True Love

Just imagine it. This woman not only stayed back, she stayed back crying. What a devoted lover she truly was! Her heart was so broken when she was bereft of her Lord. The three days' separation from Jesus was bad enough, and now it looked as though her chances of seeing Him again were fading with time. How many Christians feel such pain and distress at the slightest loss of fellowship with God? When it seems like we are no longer enjoying His manifest presence, does that set us crying?

What is the value you place on God and how well can you go on without Him? Will you still wait for Him when everyone else has walked away? Mary waited for her Lord; she placed much more value on Him than others did. They left; she stayed. She is a good example of the true believer.

When it seems our faith is becoming unpopular, all we need is the guts to keep holding on.

Though confounded, she kept praying and waiting patiently. She definitely had her fears but they were overpowered by her desire to see her Lord and Master just one more time. She was left alone. When all the big, strong men had conceded defeat, yet still she waited.

Those who take time to understand the move of the Spirit for a particular season will never be left in the back seat. They will always be at the forefront. Unique people operate on a higher frequency found only in the presence of God. There is a power that sets us on the heights of life; it is the power of God and it is found only in His presence. It often comes to us in the place of revelation, where Heaven gives information about issues that have kept men in limbo; issues that have hitherto defied all human intelligence and logic.

People who receive these revelations become the custodians of power. Such revelations are not found in public places; they come in the secret place of waiting on the Lord and hanging around the throne of His presence and grace, until God finds due expression in us.

Moses was a fugitive. He was wanted for murder in Egypt. But something happened that made him different from who he was previously. Someone stopped him in his tracks, stopped him from running away from his past, and turned him around to face it squarely — for in that horrible past lay his destiny. Moses went back to Egypt and spoke with his arch-enemy Pharaoh, one-on-one; and, from that new beginning onwards, the story was never the same again. Life grew worse for the Egyptians but better for the Israelites.

We must press on in our quest for the Lord. God might not have shown up yet; He might not have spoken a word; yet we would rather wait than turn to vagabondism. We would rather remain in the place of waiting than wander about, beating about the bush and straying far away from our purpose and appointment. Moses met God and the story had to change. He had stood in God's presence before he met Pharaoh.

A desert experience — when we feel dry spiritually and God seems to be far away — is the prelude to His showing up and bringing us to a new level. Would you care to wait for Him? Please do! Mary refused to be deprived of her time with God, even for a day, and in the midst of her tears she still carried on with her quest for Him.

Still crying, Mary looked up again into the sepulcher — and this time, it looked different. It was not empty, as it had seemed previously. What was in there was something worth seeing; something worth waiting for, all that while...

> **As she wept,** she bent over to look into the tomb **and saw** two angels in white, seated where Jesus' body had been, one at the head and the other at the foot.
>
> *John 20: 11-12*

Now, by reason of her waiting, her eyes had become enlightened. It was the same tomb but a different spectacle. If we can wait on Him, we are surely going to see something different from what others see — though we may be looking at the same thing! The eye that waits on the Lord will definitely see beyond the usual. Those who persist in spiritual matters are rewarded. It is the glory of God to conceal a thing, and the honor of kings to search it out (*Proverbs 25:2*).

The Apostles Peter and John went closer to the tomb than Mary did. They even went in. But they did not see anything. What Mary saw while waiting and eventually looking into the tomb, they could not see when they were in a hurry within the tomb. I am convinced the angels had not just arrived when Mary looked in; they must have been there all that while. We cannot get to see God when we are in a hurry. He does not do business with impatient people.

Probably the angels had decided not to reveal their presence to anyone but only those who cared to be patient enough. God is present everywhere; He is omnipresent, yet the world is full of people who are unaware of Him because they do not have time for Him. God is all around you but you may never know it until you take time to search Him out. Peter and John were standing in the same place where the Lord had lain; the napkin and the linen cloth they saw were the same ones that Jesus had been wrapped in. They stumbled in and, after a quick glance around, they stumbled out again. They didn't see what was apparent because they were in such a hurry that they had no time to wait on God.

> They asked her, "Woman, why are you crying?"
> "They have taken my Lord away," she said, "and I don't know where they have put him."
>
> *John 20:13*

The story now changes gears. Mary is not relating with men anymore but with angels. Now, she can see the unique and hear the uncommon. The angels were actually aware of her predicament because they showed they knew she was crying. But they would reveal their presence only in due season, after she had waited awhile. If you keep calling on God, one day Heaven will give you good audience. If you keep knocking on God's door, one day He will ask you to stay back.

Her patience delivered up for her what she had so strongly and tearfully desired. Her eyes were opened and she saw and spoke with angels. As it was then, so is it today: angels are not a common phenomenon but they are certainly here with us. We don't have to give up. When it seems that you have lost touch with God, all you need do is *wait*.

There may be times when you wish to pray, yet it feels as though you just can't seem to get through into God's presence. At such times, tell yourself: "This is not the time to give up, neither is it the time to play at being smart." Don't walk away either; all you need to do is *wait* on His promises.

Sometimes it might look like you have to wait for an eternity but always remember this: it might take some time but it won't be forever. In no time at all, God will show up. I can see Him reaching out to you. He is fighting your battles and it has all been set up and designed for your good.

The Next Level... a Very Different Picture

They asked her, "Woman, why are you crying?"

"They have taken my Lord away," she said, "and I don't know where they have put him."

At this, she turned around and saw Jesus standing there, **but she did not realize that it was Jesus**.

John 20: 13-14

It was morning on the *third day*, the appointed time of triumph, the time for Jesus to destroy the sting of death and proclaim victory over the grave. He had descended into the grave to fulfill a part of the redemption plan, and the time had come for Him to ascend to conclude the plan. Jesus' resurrection was the turning point, when revelations would be unveiled. Before the crucifixion, He had been the Lamb of God that took away the sins of the world; but, by virtue of His resurrection, He was now no longer a lamb but the Conqueror of Death and Hell, the Lion of the tribe of Judah, the eternal King of Glory. Mary did not know and had not met this new Jesus yet!

Coming out of the tomb, Jesus ceased to be a lamb because He had triumphed over His slaughterers and prevailed over those who smote Him. He had become Jesus the Risen Lord. The heavy stone had been sent away on sabbatical leave, and the grave refused to play host to Him any longer. Death could not hold Him captive anymore because He was now more than flesh; He now had an incorruptible body.

The resurrected Jesus was very different from the one Mary used to know before His death. He had changed and, though Mary sought for Him diligently, she could not even recognize Him when they eventually met. Why? It was because, though He still had the wounds from His crucifixion, His resurrected body was different. In fact, He had to show His disciples the holes in His hands and compel them to feel Him, to prove to them that the person they were seeing was indeed Him.

> On the evening of that first day of the week, when the disciples were together, with the doors locked for fear of the Jews, Jesus came and stood among them and said, "Peace be with you!"

After he said this, he showed them his hands and side. The disciples were overjoyed when they saw the Lord.

John 20: 19-20

When He appeared to His disciples on the shore, they did not realize at once that He was Jesus — not until He did the extraordinary, accomplishing effortlessly for them what they could not achieve all night long using human expertise:

"I'm going out to fish," Simon Peter told them, and they said, "We'll go with you." So they went out and got into the boat, but that night they caught nothing.

Early in the morning, Jesus stood on the shore, but the disciples did not realize that it was Jesus.

He called out to them, "Friends, haven't you any fish?"

"No," they answered.

He said, "Throw your net on the right side of the boat and you will find some." When they did, they were unable to haul the net in because of the large number of fish.

Then the disciple whom Jesus loved said to Peter, "It is the Lord!"

John 21: 3-7

John did not say to Peter prior to the big catch: "It is the Lord!" He must have been wondering who this person was, who showed them how to focus their efforts where they could get such overwhelming results at such short notice. Extraordinary! Until he remembered a similar incident the first time he encountered the Lord (*Luke 5: 4-10*). Before you knew it, he had exclaimed to the rest, "It is the Lord!" and, in next to no time, Peter was heading for his Master.

Peter had been the one who led the rest on the fishing escapade, to get away from their fears and disappointments in a dead Christ and Lord. It is amazing how we too, like Peter, sometimes take leave of God because we cannot imagine holding on to an unpopular faith.

A Case of Mistaken Identity

"Woman," he said, "why are you crying? Who is it you are looking for?"

Thinking he was the gardener, she said, "Sir, if you have carried him away, tell me where you have put him, and I will get him."

John 20:15

All Mary wanted was to see the Lord's dead body — when He had already risen from the dead in a glorified body! She mistook Him for the gardener at the very moment He was looking her in the eye. She had expected to see a corpse because she had seen Jesus dead and buried three days previously; but He was very much alive and could even show up in her room without opening her door or picking the locks!

Even in the midst of great reunions, we often have problems recognizing who we came to look for. Mary's questions had been answered, yet she kept looking for the "right" answers. She kept weeping and hoping that someone would someday help her, even when rescue was imminent. Sometimes, because of our "religious" or "traditional" mindset, or our preconceived notions of God and His ways, we may miss Him out when He comes to us in a new way. Religion and tradition can be the most dangerous enemies of progress.

When it seems as though God is becoming unpopular, that is the time He is about to show up strong. When it seems as though He is uncelebrated and only a few people are singing His praises, watch out because He is going to appear soon in a spectacularly different way. He is coming on a new level and, at such times, those who have waited on Him are the ones who will be the first to meet Him.

Mary took the Lord to be the gardener — just as the disciples also took Him for a ghost when He walked on water. They were scared to death because they had never seen Him in such manner before. On many occasions, we misunderstand the Lord or mistake Him for someone else because of our ignorance, tradition, religion or false ideas about Him.

Whenever you can't understand the ways of God anymore, whenever your preconceived ideas of who He is no longer suffice, whenever you can't really explain what is happening or what God is saying or driving at, you need to watch it; you are most likely on the edge of a new level. That is the time to wait upon Him and inquire of Him all the more. If you don't break faith with Him, it won't be long before He shows up and gives you new revelations of Himself.

I would encourage you to hang on. You know why? God is fast approaching. He is on His way. He really will not come late but He will come at just the right time. Your access to Him may have been delayed, but this does not imply it has been denied. He may not come according to your timing but, when He comes, that will be the best time of all.

More Importantly

> When you leave me today, you will meet two men near Rachel's tomb... They will say to you, "The donkeys you set out to look for have been found. And now your father has stopped thinking about them and is worried about you. He is asking, 'What shall I do about my son?'"
>
> *1 Samuel 10:2*

Saul went in search of his father's donkeys but at Rachel's tomb the question was, "What shall I do about my son?"

More than anything we are busy doing out there in the world, more than the ministries we are pioneering in the name of God, the major concern of the Father is us.

At Rachel's tomb, the two men's message was that the donkeys had been found but the concern now was for the missing son. God knows how to fix the problem, if there is one. He is more concerned about His missing children.

At Rachel's tomb, it was actually unnecessary to go looking for the donkeys. What was more needful was that the son be found. The most important thing in life is not human pursuits, what we want to be for ourselves or for God. The most important thing is that we enjoy unbroken fellowship with God. Stay tuned! Nothing matters more than His friendship.

The Power of Communication

> Jesus said to her, "Mary."
> She turned toward him and cried out in Aramaic, "Rabboni!" (which means Teacher).
>
> *John 20:16*

How sweet it is when God calls you by your first name! Can you imagine what it feels like? Until Jesus called her by her first name, Mary did not recognize Him. But her confusion was resolved by a simple call: "Mary!" She must have recognized her Lord's voice by the way He called her name. No one else called her that same way; no one else ever talked to her in the same manner as Jesus did.

God is consistent and His words are unchanging and infallible — yesterday, today and forever. It is impossible to change the character of His voice. You may not realize it is Him at first but, if you have been in close fellowship with Him, you will recognize His voice immediately He calls you by your name. Are you aware that God knows you by name?

It is at this juncture that many get outpaced and are deceived by the enemy. These are the people who did not have an intimate relationship with God prior to the time they found themselves at their crossroads. People who have poor communication with God will always fail at this point. Even if God speaks to them, they will not recognize His voice because they have never heard it before. And, when the devil takes advantage of the situation to speak to them, they will definitely fall for it.

If you do not have a relationship with God right now, I suggest it's high time you started talking to God one-on-one — even if it is about what you would consider to be trivial matters. Otherwise, you stand to risk missing it when you are on the edge of your next level. You could make some costly blunders if you don't realize it when He speaks to you. Communication is the lifeline of every relationship; if you don't have communication with God, you don't have power to guard against error, deception and the forces of darkness. You need to start talking to God today.

He Knows You More than You Know Him

You may be in the dark about Him but He is never in the dark about you. He can never be. We may have lost touch with Him but He never does with us. No matter what He is doing, He will never forget the names of His own. You are created in His very image. You attract Him so much.

He knows His sheep and He calls them by name (*John 10:3*). Listen, your name is engraved on the palms of His hands (*Isaiah 49:16*). You are always on His mind, notwithstanding your confusion and your tears. Seek Him early in prayer and supplication, and in sincere devotion towards Him; wait on Him patiently, looking out for Him against all odds. Before you know it, He will be calling you by name and expressing Himself in person to you.

A Beautiful Ending

> Jesus said, **"Do not hold on to me**, for I have not yet returned to the Father. **Go instead** to my brothers and tell them, 'I am returning to my Father and your Father, to my God and your God.'"
>
> Mary Magdalene went to the disciples with the news: **"I have seen the Lord!"** And she told them that he had said these things to her.
>
> *John 20: 17-18*

Oh, how I want to see the Lord too! Nothing is as beautiful as seeing Him. Mary saw the resurrected Jesus even before He had reported back to God, whilst others only saw Him after He had finished debriefing the Host of heaven. Jesus had to tell Mary not to hold onto Him because it was not proper for her to celebrate with Him before the Father had endorsed Him.

Anyone who has actually met with the Lord attains greatness in the sight of men…
Until we come into allegiance and agreement with Heaven, we cannot rise above the world.

Mary was the first person Jesus appeared to, after His resurrection; she was the first person to proclaim the good news of the Risen Savior; she was the first evangelist! How miserable Christians all over the world would be now, if Jesus had not risen from the dead; or if He had risen and we did not even know it. But thank God Mary saw Him at His resurrection! Not even the great apostles Peter and John had the privilege of preaching the first Gospel of life after death. That honor belongs to Mary alone, when she ran to tell the disciples the good news, exclaiming with exuberant joy and enthusiasm, *"I have seen the Lord!"*

If you would love to tell the world something new and true, wait on God. Would you like to run to the world with a light from God? Then you need the heart of a God-chaser, and you need a devoted and diligent spirit. God always has something new to offer to us in every season of our lives.

Every time the twenty-four elders in the Book of Revelation lifted their heads, they saw something new that drew praise and adoration from their hearts, so they kept bowing at all the manifestations of God's glory (*Revelation 4: 9-11*). God has an entirely different agenda for every season. There is always a next level and it will be revealed to the diligent and devoted.

I hear God saying to you from the Book of Isaiah:

"Behold, I will do a new thing; now it shall spring forth; **shall ye not know it?** I will even make a way in the wilderness, and rivers in the desert."

Isaiah 43:19, KJV

CHAPTER 9

God Loves Beautiful People

Now God does indeed love beautiful people and
He encourages us to be beautiful. He only differs
in His opinion of what beauty actually is...
Maybe character actually does speak louder?

The Beauty that Attracts God — and Man

If I were to tell you that God is attracted to beautiful people, how would you take it? Before you start thinking, "Blasphemy!" you should hear me out.

First, consider what the Apostle Peter wrote to Christian wives in his first epistle to God's elect. At the time of his writing, these Christian ladies were scattered throughout Pontus, Galatia, Cappadocia, Asia and Bithynia. Such Christian women are even more scattered in every nook and cranny of every nation today.

> Wives, in the same way be submissive to your husbands so that, if any of them do not believe the word, they may be won over without words **by the behavior** of their wives, when they see the purity and reverence of your lives.
>
> **Your beauty should not come from outward adornment, such as braided hair and the wearing of gold jewelry and fine clothes. Instead, it should be that of your inner self, the unfading beauty of a gentle and quiet spirit, which is of great worth in God's sight.**
>
> For this is the way the holy women of the past who put their hope in God used to make themselves beautiful. **They**

were submissive to their own **husbands,** like Sarah, who obeyed Abraham and called him her master. You are her daughters if you do what is right and do not give way to fear.

1 Peter 3:1-6

The kind of beauty the Apostle Peter was referring to, in the above passage, goes beyond haute couture clothes and the face and figure of a Miss Universe. *It entails purity, reverence and a right attitude.* He was not asking the women to worship their husbands; he only asked that they be submissive.

I firmly believe that fear of rejection is a major reason why many women get so obsessed with their appearance. Do you think you can't look good unless you conform to what fashion magazines and cosmetic surgeons define as beautiful? If you answer yes, you are very wrong. Being beautifully is about being uniquely different, as against conforming to what is in vogue.

It is true that corporal beauty fascinates people around you. There is, however, something that is capable of winning over people's hearts that is much more powerful than somatic beauty, sweet fragrances or cute looks. It is the beauty of a gentle and quiet spirit, and an obedient attitude. Why are these qualities attractive? Because man is created in the image of God; and these are the very qualities that attract God!

Yes, God is attracted to beauty — the beauty of a quiet and gentle spirit; the beauty found in a meek and obedient heart. Now, this is the kind of beauty that is being talked about here. And, if the Apostle Peter can talk about it, I am sure it is of great significance to us too. It *is* important for women to be beautiful; otherwise Peter would not have said *"your beauty"*.

Actually, I don't think anybody loves "ugly," not even the women themselves. Everybody tends to keep a look out for the beautiful ones, the beauty in every new friend; but in so doing we must be very careful that we do not miss the most vital point about beauty. It is this: when Peter used the phrase *your beauty*, he was implying that there are different kinds of beauty from which one must make a choice.

What are those choices? Peter was careful to highlight two: the kind of beauty that comes from outward adornment; and a different kind that comes from a gentle and quiet spirit — this, he said, was unfading in quality and was also the strategy holy women in the past employed to make themselves consistently gorgeous.

There is no real man who will not appreciate a pretty lady with nicely fixed hair, lovely makeup and elegant clothes on her; but you can tell that all this external beauty only moves men just for a while. It does not move God at all.

There are different kinds of beauty. There is the kind that looks good on people but it is temporal and almost every man who got married because of such beauty has ended up disenchanted. This kind of beauty results from doing up one's hair and face, and wearing jewelry and fine clothes. It is all an outward show and, yes, it does attract a lot. But if all the beauty a woman has is on the outside and there's nothing much inside her, she will definitely become a very miserable person when her external facade fades — as it must with time — and I am sure no sensible individual will love to hang out too long with anyone who lacks the vital quality that truly holds a relationship in place. The truth is anyone with a lousy spirit and an offensive attitude is most ugly, notwithstanding his or her external appearance.

Now, this does not mean we are to go around neglecting our appearance. *God is not asking us to look sloppy, as some have taught.* He is, however, telling us not to be deceived by majoring on the minor, and considering external good looks to be more important than inner beauty. The prettiest ladies in the world are not the ones parading in the Miss World pageants. Real beauties don't even show off in public... as a matter of fact, you may not recognize a beautiful person until you have spent some time with him or her.

Anybody who really wants to meet a beautiful person must be willing to look beyond the corporeal veil and also be ready to scrutinize the "bones" too. Many people have beauty that is only skin-deep; their good looks hide the ugliness buried within their "bones".

Right and Positive Attitude — Indispensable to a True Christian

Beauty has more to do with right and positive attitudes than a decorated appearance. All Christians who do not believe in the power of a positive attitude should be advised to reconsider the tenets of their faith; otherwise they are just wasting their time identifying with Christ Jesus.

Jesus believed in a right and positive attitude. Although He was God and Lord of the entire world, He was submissive to His earthly parents, Mary and Joseph, when he was a child. He was a good son. He made His parents see the reasons why He did what He did; yet He was ready and willing to obey them thereafter.

> "Why were you searching for me?" he asked. "Didn't you know I had to be in my Father's house?" But they did not understand what he was saying to them.

Then he went down to Nazareth with them and was obedient to them. But his mother treasured all these things in her heart.

Luke 2: 49-51

If we become so "heavenly-minded" that we disregard our earthly duties and responsibilities, we are only deceiving ourselves. Jesus was not only faithful in spiritual matters; He was also trustworthy in earthly concerns and submissive to earthly authorities.

When Peter came into the house, Jesus was the first to speak. "What do you think, Simon?" he asked. "From whom do the kings of the earth collect duty and taxes — from their own sons or from others?"

"From others," Peter answered.

"Then the sons are exempt," Jesus said to him. "But so that we may not offend them, go to the lake and throw out your line. Take the first fish you catch; open its mouth and you will find a four-drachma coin. Take it and give it to them for my tax and yours."

Matthew 17: 25-27

Jesus was never rude in society. He respected the law. He paid His taxes. Though He did not have money in hand to pay, it was worth getting a miracle to pay His dues. He said when questioned about taxes:

"Show me a denarius. Whose portrait and inscription are on it?"

"Caesar's," they replied.

He said to them, "Then give to Caesar what is Caesar's, and to God what is God's."

Luke 20: 24-25

This passage should not be interpreted in an unwholesome manner, as an excuse for us to compromise with the world;

rather, it sets the standard for us in attending to our social responsibilities. I am persuaded that what unique people love to do more than anything else is to concentrate on that which will attract them to God and not to men.

One thing remains true of every person God is attracted to: he or she is always in high demand among men. If you have a strong relationship with God, the world will seek you out. If you are in touch with Heaven, you will be of great value among people — whether it is to give meaning to their lives or answers to their heart-troubling questions.

Yes, God loves beautiful people — but He has His own definition of beauty. If you are not beautiful according to the definition in His glossary, He won't be attracted to you even though you might be crowned the most beautiful lady in the world or be voted the most magnificent specimen of manhood. The whole world might call you beautiful but God will judge you "very ugly" if your inner person is ugly. On the other hand, by virtue of appearance, the world might judge you ugly but God will judge you "gorgeous" if your inner person is beautiful.

Beauty and ugliness are not just skin deep. They are heart deep.

There is a beauty that fades away — and there is a beauty that does not fade. God is eternal and I am sure He always loves to establish eternal relationships with those who share His nature. God values those He regards as beautiful; He will never take their gentle and quiet spirits for granted. He places great worth on them and, in their day, they attracted Him because they consistently made themselves beautiful before Him. They were credited with having done something indispensable because they led an upright life.

The Apostle Peter held Sarah up as a very good role model to the people he was writing to. He urged them to endeavor to be like her. If we are truly strangers in this world, we have no business struggling to be like worldly people. Our business as ambassadors of God should be to carry ourselves as fitting and true representatives of His kingdom. Any man or woman who strives to "feel at home" in the world by subscribing to a worldly lifestyle does not belong to God. Let us do what is proper; it is a simple way of doing it right and living a life free from the fear of rejection.

Now, you can see that God really loves beautiful people and He encourages us to be beautiful. He only differs in His opinion of what beauty actually is. In His eyes, beauty has more to do with the components of a person's spirit, as expressed in their character and attitude, and less with the facade of physical appearance. And, God is not only attracted to beauty; He also values it greatly. The Bible says that "the unfading beauty of a gentle and quiet spirit... is of great worth in God's sight." (*1 Peter 3:4*)

CHAPTER 10

Final Words of Advice

Make an impact instead of an impression...
Avoid the shame of empty charisma.

What Do You Have?

> Now a man crippled from birth was being carried to the
> temple gate called Beautiful, where he was put every day to
> beg from those going into the temple courts. When he saw
> Peter and John about to enter, he asked them for money. Peter
> looked straight at him, as did John.
>
> Then Peter said, "Look at us!" So the man gave them his
> attention, expecting to get something from them.
>
> Then Peter said, "Silver or gold I do not have, **but what I
> have I give you.** In the name of Jesus Christ of Nazareth,
> walk."
>
> *Acts 3: 2-6*

One major reason why there is so much chaos in the world is
that only a few people understand what they have and what
they do not have, and the difference between the two. Some
people behave as though they have it all, but end up creating
most of the trouble. Others consider themselves as "have-
nots" and end up as inevitable liabilities of society.

It is important that we have a good understanding of
what we possess before we start drawing attention to
ourselves. Many people today have subjected themselves to
public ignominy due to the undue attention they attracted to
themselves. If we ask people to look up to us, we must be
ready to deliver promptly.

Peter and John must have walked past this cripple many times prior to this incident, on their way to the temple; but they did not dare approach him. Now, the reason we lack courage may be that we are not sure of what we have — or we do not even know we have the very thing that is needed to solve the problem. When you know what you have and the value of it, your countenance will display your confidence; you will be the kind who walks tall.

Don't be intimidated by what you can't do, but be proud of what you *can* do. We live in a world where many expectations are placed on us, and every day comes with its own set of demands. There will be less trouble, however, if we don't put on ourselves burdens capable of becoming clogs in our wheel.

Now, the resurrection of Jesus had made power custodians out of His disciples. One-time timid men now commanded public attention by virtue of what they had and in spite of what they did not have. Peter demanded the cripple's attention and he got it. The world out there is in dire need of effective answers and won't mind looking anywhere for them. If you claim to have something to offer, the world will come to you. If at the end of it all you don't deliver on your promises, you would have hauled public derision upon yourself. We have a lot of noisemakers but very few voices today.

But, when we receive the power that makes life work, we will not allow disability any occasion to ridicule the magnificent. Although the crippled man at the temple gate wanted something the Apostles did not have — money — they were not embarrassed to tell him they did not have what he wanted, but something better: *what he needed.*

We don't have to limit ourselves to what life demands from us. Sometimes we just have to own up and proclaim,

"There is a big difference between what you want from me and what I can offer you." This is all that's needed because in faith issues "The Giver is Sovereign, not the receiver." The Giver is God. He gives through His people.

We may not possess the answers to all the questions there are, but that does not mean we don't have something to offer. We run into a lot of trouble trying to provide answers to every question that crosses our path, when we should be providing the answers we have for the essential questions.

Peter made sure he understood what the crippled man wanted, which was different from what he needed. He also understood what he had, which was different from what he did not have. If it came to silver and gold, he was not afraid to say, "Count me out"; but when it came to the working of miracles he was bold to say, "Count me in, that's my kind of stuff!"

In most cases we don't really have what the world wants; all we have is what the world needs. You cannot afford to involve yourself in everything but you must position yourself in places where you have something tangible to offer.

I would have advised you not to go attracting attention to yourself until you have something to offer; but there is no one out there who does not already have something to offer. I will then suggest you understand what you have and what you don't, before you start calling for the world's attention. You cannot give what you don't have; and you will also not be able to give what you have if you are not aware you have it.

Find out what you have before you start thinking of giving something. Don't draw attention to yourself until you know you have something to offer. When you realize what you do have, that knowledge will give you the wisdom for what you need to do.

In Culmination

This book has been written as simply as possible,
and I hope it has been a blessing to you.

Please take note that if God decides to come to us
as big as He is, we may all run from Him.
Don't take the little things that come your way
for granted because God might be in them.
He was in the still small voice that came to Elijah
(*1 Kings 19:12*).

I love you! Take care!

About the Author

Oluwasanmi Aladeyelu is the Convener of *Truth Ministries International* (*TMI*), and a Spirit-filled end-time teacher of the Gospel Truth, blazing the trail for a later generation of anointed prophets in contemporary times. He is also the Principal Partner at *Authentic Creations and Consults Limited*. A compassionate and God-fearing author, Oluwasanmi wants to help people all over the world rise up to be the wonderful, unique men and women God has intended all of us to be. He is married to Oluwaseyi Motunrayo Olu-Aladeyelu, and they are blessed with two children, Bezaleel and Deborah.

Questions? Comments about this book?

Oluwasanmi will be glad to hear from you.

Email: kingsfits@yahoo.com

Bibliography

1. Barker, Kenneth (Editor). *The NIV Study Bible*, Zondervan Bible Publishers, 1985

2. Simox, TC. "Who Is the Angel of the Lord?" in *Israel My Glory*, Vol. 62, No. 1, January/February 2004

3. Strong, James. *Strong's Exhaustive Concordance of the Bible with Greek and Hebrew Dictionaries*, Royal Publishers, 1979

4. Williams, Derek (Editor). *New Concise Bible Dictionary*, Intervarsity Press, 1989

5. Woodbridge, John (General Editor). *Ambassadors for Christ*, Moody Press, 1994

www.ingramcontent.com/pod-product-compliance
Lightning Source LLC
Chambersburg PA
CBHW051952090426
42741CB00008B/1363